Christian
Spirituality

— an historical sketch

by George A. Lane, S.J.

Foreword by
George A. Aschenbrenner, S.J.

Afterword by
Robert T. Sears, S.J.

Loyola University Press
Chicago 60657

BX
2350.65
·L36
1984

The materials in this book—originally presented in
the form of lectures by Thomas M. Gannon, S.J.,
George W. Traub, S.J., and George A. Lane, S.J.—
were rewritten for publication by George A. Lane
and were first published in booklet form by
Argus Communications Co.

The present edition is a Loyola Request Reprint. It is
reprinted by arrangement with the author and/or the
original publisher and is now sold only by
Loyola University Press.

Portions of this book appear in revised and amplified
form in *The Desert and the City* by Thomas M. Gannon
and George W. Traub.

Stained glass by Gabriel Loire
Photo by Erne R. Frueh
Cover design by Carol Tornatore

Library of Congress Cataloging in Publication Data

Lane, George, 1934–
Christian spirituality.

Includes bibliographical references.
1. Spirituality—Catholic Church—History. 2. Catholic
Church—Doctrines—History. I. Title.
BX2350.65.L36 1984   248'.08822   83-23861
ISBN 0-8294-0450-3

Table of Contents

Foreword

CHRISTIAN SPIRITUALITY is always rooted in the experience of Jesus. As this man's love grew in fascination with this world in all its wondrous detail, his heart stretched to the length of the one he called "my dear Father." Love of this Father held him, at times, in the intimacy and wonder of quiet contemplation while, at other times, it swelled his heart with enthusiastic energy to share that love, indeed to be that love concretely for many of the people of his time. In an especially dramatic way, it was Calvary that tested and revealed the fidelity of this Son's both contemplative and apostolic love for his Father. And yet, precisely because his fidelity is a response, his own experience on Calvary, even more importantly, revealed the fidelity of a Father's love and care for his Son—and through him, for all of us. It had been a Father's love and glory that had inspired a full-hearted response in Jesus. And that response, all through his life, right to the climax on Calvary, focused and dominated all his energies, even his very person. As the "Kingdom of my dear Father" became his ALL, he became the fullest and clearest revelation we have of that Kingdom. Jesus, then, is always the attractive source and challenging exemplar for Christian spirituality.

Besides having a definite inspirational quality, the history of Christian spirituality is also instructive. To trace the response of various people down the centuries to that attractive invitation of God's love in Jesus can prevent a myopic vision of the spiritual life in our own age. An excessive absorption with the challenges and demands of the present age, without a sense of the long and varied development of spirituality, can fix our vision and limit the range of imaginative response that we feel capable of today within the Spirit of Jesus. For this reason, some familiarity with the various forms and styles of Christian spirituality as they have developed in different world contexts becomes more and more important for the mature believer. The history of Christian spirituality can give an appreciation of the basic continuity of the Spirit of Jesus revealed in and through some rather startling innovations at times—think of instances like Francis of Assisi and Ignatius of Loyola. And this appreciation can provide wise insight and imaginative hope as we continue to pass through one of the more critical upheavals and periods of radical change and discontinuity that the Church has known in her long existence.

The value of this little book will vary according to the reader's familiarity with the history of spirituality. For the beginner, it may serve as a simple, clear introduction to some of the developments within Christian spirituality. For the professional student, it can provide a good, brief, provocative review. However, the more advanced student, besides the help found here, will also want to consult the work of John Eudes Bamberger in *Cistercian Studies Series* (#4) for a fuller treatment of Evagrius Ponticus in the light of more recent research. It is also important to recognize in the book a preference for a contemporary spirituality which is more active-apostolic than monastic-apostolic. For this reason, the book gives more space to "the revolution in spiritual thinking and practice brought about by St. Ignatius." (p. 42). This would seem appropriate since this Ignatian spirituality, which developed as an attractive alternative to the previous valid monastic forms, has left its stamp on most of contemporary spirituality.

Christian spirituality is part of the story of the human heart's longing for sanctity. I am glad that this brief version of the Christian story is being reprinted. Through it may the awesome holiness of God continue to stir the deepest longing and response in all our hearts for the justice and joy of sanctity.

George A. Aschenbrenner, S.J.

The Hallowed Eve of All Saints
1983

Introduction

A RENEWED INTEREST IN SPIRITUALITY is part of the total renewal that is taking place in the Church as a result of the Second Vatican Council. The Church's effort to achieve a deeper understanding of herself and the roles of the various clerical, religious, and lay groups within her forms a backdrop against which a renewal in spirituality is taking place.

In recent years there has been a growing interest in the psychological aspects of spirituality and religious life. Much of this interest has been directed toward the understanding of the unique human person who seriously tries to live a spiritual life. This psychological dimension has ushered in a much more humane approach to many aspects of religious life which was much needed to counter the ultra-mechanical piety of the 19th and early 20th centuries.

But besides the psychological dimension of renewal, there is a theological dimension. The theological import of such theologians as Häring, Schillebeeckx, Rahner, and others must be carefully studied and taken into account if we are to arrive at a valid contemporary spirituality.

We must never forget that the chief problem confronting any kind of renewal is how to balance the changing with the changeless, how to balance the demands of contemporaneity with the treasures of the past. This is the problem

1

we face in attempting to formulate a spirituality which is at once vital for our time and solidly grounded in the best traditions of the past.

Keeping in mind, then, this basic problem of renewal, it will be valuable to make an historical-theological survey of Christian spirituality. Why do we take this approach? In so much of the work of Vatican II the direction of renewal has been solidly based upon and influenced by the past. We look to the sources of Christian life and try to discover how it has developed.

In much the same way, Vatican II urges religious communities to look to their origins and to understand the original inspiration of their founders. In this way they can be true to their traditions and at the same time chart out a program of vital renewal. In short, Teilhard de Chardin has summed it up in *The Future of Man* when he says, "Everything is the sum of the past; nothing is comprehensible except through its history."[1] Failure to grasp the historical perspective so often condemns people to relive the mistakes of the past.

How can we arrive at an authentic program for seeking union with God in our present time in our particular way of life within the Church? Basically we have to keep the past and the future in mind in order to arrive at a valid spirituality for the present. We must preserve the best traditions from the past and look to the future for our goals; from these two perspectives we can address the present in a much more effective way.

In a broad sense spirituality may be described as a way to holiness; but more technically, spirituality is man's possession by God in Christ through the Holy Spirit. There is, then, only one spirituality because there is only one Christ; but when the means of union with God become concretized, various different styles of approach appear. A particular style of approach to union with God is then called a spirituality. John Courtney Murray, S.J. has said that God would have each man wholly to be His witness, but not necessarily a witness to the whole of Him. Only the Church, as the community of the faithful, in many-splendored variety can really bear witness to the whole counsel of God.[2]

Now this distinction between man's fundamental union with God and the various styles of approach to it has very important ramifications. At any given time and place in history, society challenges men and women differently, and therefore challenges them to respond to God differently. These challenges have brought forth responses from extraordinary men and women—the hermits of the East, the monks of the West, Basil, Athanasius, Origen, Jerome, Augustine, Benedict, Dominic, Francis, and Ignatius to name only a very few. So penetrating was their vision of the relevance of Christ to their society that they were followed by large numbers of Christians who wished to share their vision and their way of life.

There is a distinction between the basic world-view (or God-view) of these great men, their vision, and certain techniques used by their followers to implement the vision. The vision is unchangeable, but the techniques used to implement and institutionalize it are intrinsically and necessarily adaptive.

In the history of the Church certain structural elements remain constant throughout the history of spirituality although they may be implemented differently at different times. If we are going to have an authentically Christian spirituality for our own time, we have somehow to provide for the perennial elements like prayer, penance, mortification, and apostolic activity.

There is much talk today of searching the writings of the 20th century, our own novelists and thinkers, to find a contemporary spirituality. This will undoubtedly be helpful, but it will only be by probing the mystery of Christ as He is transmitted to us through the history of the believing Church that we will find an authentic spirituality. Accordingly, our effort will be to distinguish the vision of the great leaders in the Church from certain intrinsically adaptive techniques, and try to fit the enduring values to the spirit and conditions of our own time.

A final word of caution. We are going to examine a theology of the spiritual life. Now there is a distinction between a systematic understanding of the Christian response and the lived experience of the spirituality. Ideally they should coincide and infuse one another. But the problem is that the lived experiences of the great founders of religious orders is a unique thing, and it dies out with the people who have had that experience. It is not the lived experience which stays on to influence us; it is the theology or the way that experience was explained and interpreted that survives. For example, some of the problems we might have about the hermits in the East and the monks in the desert were not necessarily problems for them, but they are for us. This is partly because we do not have the same vision that they did, but we do have the systematic explanation of their way of life and this is what influences us. We cannot criticize their life experience; but we can criticize and evaluate their articulation or explanation of it in order to discover what may be valid for our own purposes.

Protest and Renunciation in the East

IN THE HISTORY OF CHRISTIAN SPIRITUALITY the Eastern monastic movement is one of the most difficult for us to understand. We feel so far removed from these people; and what they did seems at times so bizarre as to be hardly imitable, although it inspires us in an abstract sort of way. It is rather difficult today to appreciate the man fleeing from the world into the quiet sandy desert to come into contact with God.

But in order to approach the Eastern monastic movement as well as the whole of spirituality, we have to recognize a certain basic yearning for self-surrender that is present in every individual person. This yearning rises at times to a passion; it is something of an instinct which we cannot fully explain. It is a drive that leads many people, almost in spite of themselves, to moments of heroic decision to give their lives to others. There are few people to whom there does not sometime occur a vision of a nobler life and a better existence.

There are many ways of explaining this instinct, an escape from a restrictive and repressive conscience, a yearning for the infinite, a search for meaning, the desire for God.

This yearning for self-surrender is something we take as a given with the human situation. It is the basic presupposition to which Christ appeals in the Gospels. For the person who accepts Christ as the Lord and commits himself entirely to Him, this self-surrender is not a counsel, it is an imperative call of the Master. "Anyone who prefers father or mother to me is not worthy of me . . . . And he who does not take up his cross and come follow me is not worthy of me."[3] Now passages like this in the New Testament are very hard to interpret from an *a priori* standpoint, but it is very easy to understand them if we see them in the light of the Church and in the history of the people who have done this sort of thing.

This is what was underneath the Eastern monastic response. The form of this surrender has changed through the years; but its starting point has always been the same, an acceptance of and a commitment to the Risen Lord. These people believed wholeheartedly as they read the Gospel that the only way to respond authentically to Christ was to get away from the din of the world and to go out to the desert to find Him there. One had to flee the city of sin in order to find God, the pure God who was wholly other, wholly apart, and wholly transcendant to this city of sinful men.

Unfortunately some of the bizzare practices of the monks often overshadow the real essence of their life and work. We cannot let these peculiarities influence our understanding of the Eastern monk, because coupled with certain unusual practices was the motivation of protest and renunciation which permeated the entire Eastern movement. These men felt the world was evil. The only way they could achieve union with Christ was to protest the evil world and renounce these evil temptations.

But underlying the whole Eastern monastic movement we must not fail to notice a captivating enthusiasm. These men were utterly convinced that theirs was a magnificent vocation. They did not condemn others, but looked upon them as hopelessly caught in the turmoil of the world. They had made a great discovery, found the only way to profound union with God. This enthusiasm comes out in St.

Anthanasius' life of St. Anthony the Hermit. Anthony had lived forty years in the desert, and when people went out to visit him

> He came forth as from some shrine, like one who has been initiated in the sacred mysteries, and filled with the spirit of God. Then, for the first time, he was seen outside the fort by those who came to him. They were amazed to see that his body was unchanged, for it had not become heavy from lack of exercise, nor worn from fasting and struggling with the evil spirits; he was just as they had known him before he had secluded himself. The temper of his soul, too, was faultless, for it was neither straightened as if from grief, nor dissipated by pleasure, nor was it strained by laughter or melancholy. He was not disturbed when he saw the crowd, nor elated at being welcomed by such large numbers; he was perfectly calm, as befits a man who is guided by reason and who has remained in his natural state. (The state in which Adam and Eve were created, but which was damaged by the fall.) Through him the Lord healed many of those who were suffering in body and freed them from evil spirts.[4]

This is only one of the many passages which bear witness to the enthusiasm the Eastern monks conveyed to their contemporaries.

What were the conditions which made this type of response to the Gospel intelligible or even necessary? The background of the early Church and the history of the decline of the Empire is important to know in order to fully understand Eastern monasticism. In its earliest days the Church was looked upon as a Jewish sect and was treated accordingly with tolerance. But as the Christians became more numerous, toleration diminished and persecution began. Martyrdom then became the pinnacle of Christian renunciation. It was a way in which a man could say, "I am renouncing myself, taking up my cross, and literally following Christ."

But when the period of martyrdom and persecutions was over, how could a person reach the pinnacle of Christian perfection? Martyrdom had been the ideal, and now there were no martyrs. One had to search for another ideal. The life of the hermit soon became this ideal. The writings of the period show that going into hermitage was another way of reaching the same height of perfection as martyrdom.

Besides this, we have the peculiar effect on the Church of the conversion of Constantine in 303. In a way the whole Empire became Christian with him, and when large groups of people flood into an organization, the original quality is bound to be diluted. The Christians were inundated by time-servers and half-converted pagans. At one time Christians had laid down their lives for truth, now they slaughtered one another to gain the prizes of the Church, and the Church became a vehicle for power.

Now it was against all of this that monasticism was a protest. It was not just against the world, but it was especially against the world in the Church. In this connection too, it is important to remember that monasticism was originally a lay movement. In fact, the monks were quite anti-clerical, as some of the Jewish prophets were anti-clerical; Amos and Hosea, for instance, condemned the merely cultic priests who did not preach justice and love, but became fully en-. meshed in the power structure of the state. The monks were anti-clerical in this sense; it was part of their prophetic witness. They were protesting the world in the Church, and accordingly the monastic movement is to be seen not so much within the Church as alongside of it.

Now monastic flight from the world was not a sudden thing; it evolved gradually. The early monks lived in the city, stayed in their houses more than their neighbors, and did not go out to the desert until somewhat later on. One of the reasons for eventually going out to the desert was the belief that there one could encounter the devil or God in pure form.

At first individuals went out alone to the desert hermitage; but because living alone is very difficult and people with like interest naturally band together, in the course of time hermits united into cenobitic communities. We read that in the fourth century one might find as many as five thousand hermitages scattered over a single mountainside in Egypt.

Another factor that contributed to the "flight from the world" was the belief of some that God could not be found among men. The Abbot Marcus asked the Abbot Arsenius, "Wherefore do you flee from us; and the old man said, 'God knows that I love you, but I cannot be with God and with men—a thousand and a thousand thousand angelic powers have one will, but men have many. Therefore I cannot send God from me and come and be with men.' "[5]

The corrupt and corroding city of man at this time was another factor that prompted the withdrawal to the city of God in the desert. The Empire was decaying; and what remedy could heal the weakened manhood, bad finance, and lowered ideals that were working their inevitable destruction on organized society? Withdrawal seemed a quite plausible solution.

But the ideals of monasticism are still operative today. Dom Hubert Van Zeller points out that it is "not in outward activities that the strength of monasticism lies. The direct contribution is not and never has been the main thing. The main thing has been the indirect contribution made by prayer and penance . . . the monk who loves God perfectly is fulfilling every obligation which in Christian charity he owes to his neighbor."[6] Now there is always need for protest, renunciation, and solitude. The question that we musk ask is, what form should protest, renunciation, and solitude take today?

In conclusion we have to ask some diffucult questions of early Eastern monasticism. Is this not an aristocratic spiritualilty, an elitist movement for a few? The monks seemed to be a breed set apart in favored conditions in an isolated environment. Can anyone afford the luxury of an elitist spirtuality today? And does Christ preach an elitist spirituality in the Gospel? It seems not. There is also the problem of what we might call the essentialist view of man, man made up of distinct component parts with mind warring against the flesh. With such a view one might go off to the desert to fight himself, to conquer the flesh definitively. But such a person will usually find that he is his own worst enemy. He creates more problems in isolation than he ever would have found in contact with other people. Not only does one run the risk of exposing himself to greater conflict that he would have found among people, but the problems will have been of his own making. And then in face of the social difficulites of the time, perhaps it was easier to abandon the sinking ship of the Church rather than try to guide it into port.

The contemporary question, however, which we must ask ourselves is how can we preserve the ideals of protest and renunciation of this way of life and sift out the ideals and customs which have come down to us and are not suited to our age or mentality.

The Ideal
of Contemplation

IN THIS CHAPTER we wish to focus our attention on the notion of prayer prevalent among certain Eastern desert monks in the third and fourth centuries. We will concern ourselves with only one school of the spiritual life and one very limited style of prayer. What we are referring to is commonly known as the Origenist school. The name is taken from the great Origen, but the doctrine is not to be confused with his at all. Of the two groups within Egyptian monasticism, the Origenist-Alexandrians and the Copts, the former were far more influential than the more numerous Copts simply because they used Greek, the literary and scientific language of the whole eastern Mediterranean. The Origenist writings were widely circulated and have survived to influence almost all of later Christian spirituality.

It will help us understand this movement if we have some idea of the intellectual currents circulating in Alexandria in the third and fourth centuries. A fairly intelligent person at that time would have been acquainted with a conglomeration of Platonism, Stoicism, Gnosticism, Manichaeism, and Neoplatonism—all adding up to a certain dualism, spirit in opposition to matter. The spiritual human soul emanates from a supreme Intelligence, the One, and is imprisoned in the material, evil body. This imprisonment of the soul accounts for all the evil in the world; and so the soul must fight the body, overcome it, and strive to reach a state of impassivity where the soul is insensitive to all things of this world. The principal task of the soul is to escape, release itself, and reascend to its place of origin in the One.

So the educated Alexandrian of this time might be involved in a struggle against his body in order to bring it under control, overcome it, and finally achieve that state which was called *apatheia,* a state of total insensitivity, an oblivion to all material things, especially one's own body and its needs in so far as this is possible. This type of asceticism is directed towards controlling one's body, bringing it under submission, and transcending it.

In addition to the ascetical practices leading to this state of *apatheia,* there is a final stage of contemplative life, a state of *gnosis* which is a special type of knowledge. This final stage reaches a level of contemplation wherein the soul achieves total freedom from the body and fixes its attention solely on spiritual realities. The mind contemplates the One and thereby anticipates its state of reabsorption into the One which is its final destiny. The two processes of this asceticism, *apatheia* and *gnosis,* were both part of the intellectual milieu in third and fourth century Alexandria.

For the early Christians in this part of the world it was a great problem to maintain the purity of the Gospel in the face of these philosophical currents. It was not surprising that a great school and a series of great teachers developed in Alexandria who attempted to develop through scholarship, teaching, and writing a synthesis of these pagan intellectual currents and Christianity. What was good in this philosophical tradition could be drawn into a Christian spirituality and be put at the service of the Christian faith. What was incompatible could be discarded.

The culmination of this synthesis came in the great Origen who lived from 185 to 252 A.D. We have already distinguished this man Origen from the Origenist school which unfortunately took its name from him. Origen was a magnetic personality who drew many people around him. His life was marked both by great austerities and an immensely energetic devotion to the apostolate. He effected the most successful synthesis of pagan philosophy and Christianity.

Origen proposed a doctrine of Christocentric asceticism and mysticism. Right away we notice the shift in Origen's thinking away from the pagan views of the time. Human perfection for him was not to be found in knowledge but in love and the works of charity. Renunciation, asceticism, and contemplation were not for Origen the end of the spiritual life, but means for conquering evil inclinations and achieving a perfect love of Christ who is the actual end and aim of spirituality.

Origen certainly had an influence on those who fled into the desert about a half century after his death. But when his great Christian synthesis was taken up by the desert monks, it proved too delicate and it succumbed to the influence of the pagan philosophical milieu, especially in the hands of Evagrius of Pontus.

Evagrius is a sort of mystery figure who is referred to again and again by the various chroniclers of Christian history. After his doctrines were condemned by the Council of Alexandria in 399, his writings continued to be circulated for centuries under the names of Nilus of Ancyra and St. Basil and other orthodox teachers of the time.

Evagrius was a great enthusiast. He came from Asia Minor near the Black Sea. In his early life he was tried by temptations against chastity, and in the face of these he decided to flee to the desert near Jerusalem where there was a thriving series of monastic communities. He did not remain long near Jerusalem, however, for he was soon attracted to Egypt by the stories and legends of the desert monks there. He spent the last twenty years of his life teaching and writing in the desert outside of Alexandria.

Evagrius lived until 399, and it was only a few months after his death in that year that his Origenist doctrines were condemned.

The doctrine of Evagrius is that of Origen with most of the essentials of Christianity removed. The importance of the man's work is that he systematized many elements of asceticism as they were preached and practiced in his circles. There are basically two aspects to his doctrine, that of the active life and of the contemplative life. These terms have special meanings and are not to be confused with our contemporary understanding of them.

The active life can be summed up as virtue achieved through the analysis and methodical avoidance of vice. In fact, Evagrius was the first to come up with the doctrine of the deadly sins. He proposed eight of them. The methodical ridding of the soul of vice was carried on in order to achieve the negative goal of *apatheia*. Without this insensitivity to the world it would be impossible for a person to move on to the contemplative life.

Once perfect control over the body and material things is achieved, one moves to the contemplative stage where another kind of asceticism takes place, that of the mind. The mind is systematically purged of all images, symbols, and concepts, so that eventually it reaches a certain unconsciousness, *anaesthesia*. It is this unconsciousness that brings the very highest type of knowledge, knowledge in pure contact with God apart from any human or worldly content. Hence the object of the contemplative life is to gradually empty the mind in order for God to come in and fill it. And this, of course, is the very perfection of all Christian and human life.

This concept of contemplation leads to Evagrius' understanding of prayer, a raising of the *mind* to God. Every single thing is to be sacrificed for the pursuit of prayer. "Go," he says, "sell all that you have and take up the Cross; deny yourself so that you can pray without distraction."[7] Or again, "if you would pray worthily, deny yourself continually; if you undergo trials of all sorts, accept your lot philosophically out of love for prayer."[8] Prayer is a chance for the soul to escape at least temporarily from the body. Evagrius says, "when your intelligence goes out of the body and rejects all thoughts that come from sense and memory and bodily humors and is filled with awe and joy, then it is allowable to think that you are close to the confines of prayer."[9]

So prayer is an impassive state of existence free of all feeling and emotion. Prayer is an emptying of the mind. "Even if the intelligence raises itself above the contemplation of bodily nature, it has not yet perfect contemplation of God because it can still mingle with the intelligibles and share in their multiplicity."[10] Finally, prayer for Evagrius is an angelic activity. "You wish to pray?" he asks; "depart from here below and have your dwelling continually on high, not in name only but by a kind of angelic practice and by a knowledge more divine."[11]

Lastly it is important to note that the active life and the contemplative life in the doctrine of Evagrius do not intermingle with one another. One goes through a process of purification and gradually achieves a state of insensitivity. Only then is it possible to pass on to the contemplative life, and it is in this state that prayer is described as an emptying of the mind in order that God may be encountered free from any trace of what is human or wordly. This Evagrian doctrine of prayer is, in fact, a cult of contemplation. "Pure" prayer and perfection are identified. And this prayer (not the love and service of Christ) is the goal of the Christian life.

The two most important transmitters of the Evagrian teaching are John Cassian and Pseudo-Dionysius. John Cassian was a close associate of Evagrius in the Egyptian desert. When Origenism was condemned in 399, Cassian fled for his life and gradually made his way to the West. There in southern France he established two religious communities, one for men and one for women. Most important, perhaps, he wrote two famous works, *The Institutes* and the *Conferences*. In these books Cassian transmitted Evagrius' doctrine to the West in a somewhat tempered form. However, the ideal of angelic contemplation was still presented as the goal and perfection of the Christian life. Anything else, any time taken from contemplation, was taken from God.

The other transmitter, Pseudo-Dionysius, comes somewhat later. According to his own testimony, Dionysius was a confidant of the Apostles, was present at the crucifixion of Christ, was with St. John at the time the Apocalypse was composed; he heard St. Paul make his famous speech in the Areopagus, and he recounts many other such personal experiences which are obviously wide of the truth. One important fact, however, is that after St. Augustine he is the most frequently quoted source of Thomas Aquinas. This is an indication of the influence he had upon the thinking of the Middle Ages.

As far as scholars have been able to determine, Pseudo-Dionysius lived around 600 A.D. and was probably a hermit in the deserts of Syria. His contribution to the ideas of Evagrius consists of a refining of techniques. How was one to achieve the ideal of contemplation? The work of Pseudo-Dionysius was an attempt to transfer a "spiritual" ideal into a program of mystical psychology.

The negative method of theology is the key to the program. This consists of looking at the things of this world, finding various perfections in them, and attributing these perfections to God. However, all that is imperfect in this world, evil, sin, and any imperfection, is denied of God. Pseudo-Dionysius transferred this method to the psychological realm so that in order to achieve mystical union with God in contemplation, one goes through a carefully calculated set of steps for gradually bringing the mind under control and emptying it of all its worldly contents.

Because of Dionysius' supposed authority as an intimate of the Apostles, his works enjoyed great popularity in the West; and he supplied a vocabulary which would later be used by such mystics as Meister Eckhart and John of the Cross.

The Origenist school itself was very limited, but its influence has been immeasureable down through the centuries. In this spirituality all is to be sacrificed for prayer, that is, contemplation, which is the raising of the intelligence above and beyond all things to God. This is the highest of all human activities; to achieve this is to be perfect, for it makes man like the angels; it effects heaven on earth. It is clear, however, that this style of prayer is more strongly determined by the Alexandrian philosophical tradition than it is by Sacred Scripture.

It is interesting to note, too, that this school of spirituality developed somewhat apart from the ordinary Christian community in the midst of a people who wanted to separate themselves from the Alexandrian Church in protest against it.

There are many questions which arise: should men do what angels do? Should man on earth do what he will do in heaven? Or more fundamentally, is heaven totally different from earth, a kind of pure gazing? And will heaven be a purely intellectual exercise where our bodies (despite the orthodox doctrine of the resurrection of the body) have no place at all? It is perhaps not fair to pass judgment on this movement. At the same time it would be a serious mistake if we uncritically accepted some of these techniques and ideals of spirituality.

We must ask ourselves where our notion of prayer comes from. Is it a bit Evagrian? Does it have to be de-Alexandrianized? While prayer itself remains an essential of the Christian life, the precise form it takes in any culture must be suited to the mentality of that age and it must also conform to the principal of the Gospel.

Benedictine Spirituality

WE SHIFT OUR ATTENTION NOW from the East to the West, and we want to describe the Benedictine ideal of spirituality. We will find it conditioned by a simpler, less sophisticated culture in the West, a more biblical notion of God, and the grace and personality peculiar to St. Benedict.

Benedict, the founder of Western monasticism, was born in Nursia in Umbria around the year 480, and he lived until 547. Early in his youth Benedict went to Rome to study, but after a while he left the city because he could not live the Christian life as he wanted to in the midst of the corruption there. Rome at this time was the scene of barbarian invasions, social breakdown, disorder and confusion. So Benedict left the city and became a hermit; he lived alone for three years on Mt. Subiaco.

After this three year eremetic period, Benedict went to a place called Vicovaro where a number of other monks gathered around him. Benedict tried to get his companions to lead a more fervent monastic life. What form this took is unsure, but his companions did not like his ideas, and they tried to poison him. This incident terminated Benedict's first cenobitic experience. Needless to say, Benedict was well acquainted with the disorderly varieties of the monastic life which were then prevalent both in the East and West. Benedict eventually went to another place on Mt. Subiaco and began to set up new communities. He established twelve different monasteries there, and finally he went to Monte Cassino around the year 528. There he founded the famous monastery and wrote the Holy Rule in the last years of his life.

In the beginning of his Rule, Benedict specifies that he is not describing a way of life for anchorites, gyrovagues, stylites, or any other type of free-lance monk who was on the scene at this time. He makes a definite break from all the peculiarities that had crept into Eastern and Western monasticism.

What was the original form of the Benedictine life and its spiritual ideal? Aiden Cardinal Gasquet in his commentary on the Holy Rule says, "Benedict regarded monastic life . . . as a systematized form of life on the lines of the Gospel counsels of perfection, to be lived for its own sake and as a full expression of the Church's true and perfect life—the perfect liturgical life and that of perfecting the individual soul."[12] We note especially the personal sanctification, the Gospel counsels of perfection, and liturgical life in community. The spiritual ideal described here is the perfecting of the individual soul through the perfect living of the Christian life in community.

Life in community is essential for Benedict. The apostolate of the monk is entirely indirect. "The monk who loves God perfectly is fulfilling every obligation which in Christian charity he owes to his neighbor."[13]

This love of God can be practiced right within the monastery, which should then strive to be a perfectly self-sufficient institution. "The monastery, if possible, should be so constructed that all things necessary may be contained within it, water, a mill, a garden, a bakery, and the various workshops, so that there may be no need for the monks to go abroad, for this is not at all healthful for their souls."[14]

A direct apostolate of service to the neighbor was not part of the original vision of Benedict.

Another essential point in the original plan is that monastic life is organized according to rule. Benedict did not want each monk going his own way; the Holy Bible would govern and determine the way of life in the monastery. The abbot himself was under the rule, not over it. This counteracted the unorganized and often disorderly lives of many monks at that time.

The Rule also prescribed a certain moderation and discretion in all things. A life of controlled simplicity with sufficient food and clothing was noticeably different from the often outlandish austerities of some of the Eastern monks. Moderation and discretion are essential and are often noted as characteristic elements of Benedict's way of life.

The Holy Rule also prescribed the daily order in the monastery; it did not encourage individuality, rather community living with the most of the monks doing the same thing at the same time. Benedict had the older monks sleep with the younger ones to be sure they all got up when the rising bell rang. Everyone came to the choir at the same time; and if someone was late, he had to sit in a special place conspicuous to all.

Stability was another important aspect of the Benedictine life. The social flux and disorder of the times was surely one determining factor in this element of monastic life. Monks would vow stability to one monastery and then live out their lives in that same house. Stable institutions were not common in southern Europe at this time. In this context stability was a very valuable thing.

What sort of social structure existed in the monastic community? First, there was the abbot. He was the father of the community, the superior; and he was permanently assigned in order to give the continuity, stability, unity, and consistency desired in the monastery. Obedience was vowed to the abbot as to Christ.

The monastery itself was thought of as a home. The

vow of stability made it a personal stable society. And it is interesting to note that Benedict's Rule is drawn up for one monastery, not for a monastic order. It was only later that the Benedictines were considered an order. This idea of the monastery as a home replaced all the peculiarities of anchorites' huts, stylites' columns, and pilgrims' wanderings from one place to another.

Since the monks thought of themselves as a family, their numbers were restricted to keep the monastery within family proportions. When they grew too numerous, some branched off and started a new foundation.

It is important to recall that all the monks were originally laymen. Chapter 62 of the Holy Rule says clearly, "If an abbot desires to have a priest or a deacon ordained for his community, let him choose from among his monks one who is worthy to perform the priestly office."[15] But the priest, if there is to be one in the community, is to have no preference or precedence over anybody else.

Daily life in the monastery consisted of a rhythmic balance of three elements: liturgical prayer, manual labor, and *lectio divina.*

Liturgical prayer is chiefly the chanting of the Divine Office in choir according to the canonical hours. This is an essential element of monastic life, and it is the element which sets the rhythm for the whole monastic life. A good part of the Holy Rule is devoted to prescriptions as to how the Divine Office is to be sung.

The second element is daily manual labor. This work aspect of Benedictine life is an integral part of the daily order of the monastery. Benedict preferred that the work be farm work. The purpose of this work was to avoid idleness and to take care of the material needs of the monastery. Manual labor was a physical exercise element too that was to be integrated into the balanced rhythm of community living. This is what Benedict envisioned. We notice that the work element in Benedictine life was not conceived to be apostolic service. It was not intended to serve the needs of the Church directly nor was it mission oriented. It was simply an element in the daily order for the good of the monks and the community.

The third element in the daily life of a monk was the *lectio divina.* This is a quiet prayerful reading of sacred scripture. "To read sacred scripture was in fact to meditate on it and the process could easily turn into prayer, and prayer which could beome contemplative; but this would be a gift of God to be waited for and not sought."[16] This, of course, is radically different from the contemplative prayer ideal of Origenism. This is not trying to be angelic; it is not like trying to be in heaven while still on earth. It is a much more realistic type of prayer. Benedict himself does not use the word contemplation anywhere in his Rule. For Cassian a conscious seeking of the angelic life was the ideal and aim of the spiritual life; not for Benedict. For Benedict perfection is not in tranquillity and contemplation, rather it is in charity, humility, and obedience in community life.

Even today many can look at this way of life and see it as a beautiful and practical ideal of the spiritual life which is definitely livable under the conditions which can be set up and determined within a monastery.

Very early in Benedictine history definite departures were made from the way of life we have just described. These departures from the original concept can be viewed either as a deviation from or a development of the Benedictine way of life.

The first departure came when Pope Gregory the Great called upon St. Augustine and the Benedictines to evangelize England. When the pope desired to send missionaries to England, the only really organized group of men whom he could call upon were the Benedictines. The pope called on them and thus initiated the great evangelization of England, and eventually much of northern Europe by the great Benedictine saints Augustine of Canterbury, Benet, Bede, Boniface, and many more.

The missionary apostolate called for the priest-monk.

And the response to this demand eventually changed the Benedictines from a lay to a predominantly clerical institute. Preparation for the priesthood then introduced the need for teachers, books, learning, libraries, and the whole ideal of study as work in the monastery. The work element in the monastery began to change from farm work to intellectual work. Classes which originally served for the training of the priest-monk eventually developed into schools for extern students. The great tradition of the monastery school developed during the Middle Ages. Teaching, study, and manuscript work grew to such proportions that they almost entirely displaced the manual work, and lay help was secured to work the fields of the monasteries.

Under the missionary demand of the Church, the spiritual ideal shifts from personal santification for the individual to apostolic ministry in the service of the Church.

Are all of these changes departures from or legitimate developments of the Benedictine way of life? Dom Hubert Van Zeller and others view these changes as contrary to the original ideal. Yet other Benedictines think they are genuine developments of it. One needs a good working theory of renewal and development in order to evaluate such changes as these.

It will be helpful to consider briefly two major Benedictine reform movements, the Cluniac and the Cistercian reforms of the 10th and 12th centuries respectively.

The Cluniac reform chiefly concerned certain governmental and liturgical aspects of the Benectine life and organization. During the feudal age many monasteries developed large and valuable land holdings. Abbots came to control vast resources of wealth and powers, and this caused serious troubles and disorders. The Cluny reform created a centralized federation of monasteries by affiliating smaller houses with larger ones. Ultimately there were fifteen hundred monasteries in western Europe affiliated with Cluny. The effect of this was to shake off the secular and episcopal control of the monasteries. It freed them from the political involvements in which they had become entangled.

Another important aspect of the Cluny reform was a greatly increased emphasis on the liturgy. Long, elaborate, and magnificently performed liturgical ceremonies were developed. The Divine Office grew beyond what St. Benedict had prescribed and the prayer element grew to such proportions that it almost eliminated the work element in Benedictine life, and the original balance was lost.

The Cistercian reform began around 1100 and was chiefly an effort to return to the original monastic life as prescribed by St. Benedict. The reformers wanted a literal interpretation of the Holy Rule. This meant removing the accretions to the Divine Office which had come in with Cluny. It meant a return to primitive manual labor in the fields, preferably farm work over manuscript work or teaching; a return to the simple poor life of interior personal sanctification; and a return to solitude, locating the monastery in a remote place. The Cistercians cut off many of the sources of property, wealth, and power which had come to many of the monasteries.

In conclusion the spiritual ideal of the Benedictine Rule is achieved through the living of the perfect Christian life in a regular balanced cycle of meditative reading of the sacred scripture interspersed with work and the whole life regulated by the chanting of the Divine Office in choir. The Benedictines consider that any overemphasis or under-emphasis on any one of these elements is a departure from the ideal of St. Benedict. What is noticeable is a certain polarity in reform and renewal and this is pertinent today. One pole in the effort of renewal is the spirit and the words and the writings of the founder. The other pole in reform is the demands of the times, and the demands of the Church in light of the Holy Spirit. These two interact, but the question remains, how are they to be balanced harmoniously so as to preserve both values.

The Mendicant
Transition

IN THE OPENING YEARS of the thirteenth century religious life in the Church entered upon a great revolution. Without changing its basic principles of poverty, chastity, and obedience, it sought to work out its ideals no longer by withdrawing from men, but by seeking to serve them directly. Up to this time the highest religious life had been identified with a retreat from the world, retiring like St. Bruno to some Grande Chartreuse where in a rarer air, far from the noise and bustle of the world, men could save their souls and develop a height of virtue and piety. But the Franciscan and Dominican friars were essentially different; they were orders of social laborers; they were to go about in the world doing good.

What we might call the mendicant transition accompanied a general shift in western Europe from a predominantly rural agrarian culture to an urban commercial culture. Feudalism was giving way to the medieval city; merchants and artisans emerged as the nucleus of the new middle class; and the universities were founded in the cities. The mendicant orders of St. Francis and St. Dominic arose to meet the religious challenges of this new age.

Other factors were woven into the fiber of the times. The Crusades had given the western world a taste of the luxury of the East, the silks, satins, and spices. An attachment to luxurious living even spread among the clergy and monks. And the romantic movement was beginning in southern Europe; troubadours and love stories flourished. Paralleling this was the emergence of more sentimental devotions within the Church. Hymns like "Jesu dulcis memoria" reflect the sweet flavor of this period. The humanity of Jesus and the Blessed Virgin played an important part in the developing spirituality of the age. The Passion of Christ, the Blood of Christ, His five wounds, and many other devotions centered around the humanity of Christ developed in the spirituality of this time.

Besides the social factors which paved the way for the mendicant response, there were theological factors too. The friars were founded to combat a rising tide of heresy at the time. Ronald Knox speaks of the "underworld of the Middle Ages."[17]It was made up of two currents, the Catharist movement and the Waldensian movement; both of which contributed to the Albigensian heresy.

The Catharist heresy, very much like the Manichaean heresy, held that material things were evil—the body, the state, the visible church. Therefore bodily asceticism and fasting almost to the point of death were considered right and proper. Given the context of wealth and luxury from the Crusades, this movement made sense to many people and stimulated a great enthusiasm among them.

Side by side with this was the Waldensian movement, named after Peter Waldo of Lyons. In the famine year of 1176, he gave away his property and tried to live out the very letter of the commandments and the poverty which he thought Christ proposed in the Gospels. The Waldensians were at first orthodox and the message which they proclaimed was quite legitimate; but they were forced into heresy. The failure of the Church to see what the Waldenses were trying to introduce forced them to go too far and eventually they wound up in heresy. They developed into a sizeable movement, and their distinguishing marks were poverty, bible reading, and itinerant preaching.

A glimpse into the history of this time shows that these people were reacting to specific evils in the Church and in society. The Dominican prior of Louvain, Thomas of Chantimpre wrote, "I met on the street an abbot with so many horses and so large a retinue that if I had not known him I would have taken him for a duke or a count. Only the addition of a circlet on his brow would have been needed."[18]

It was in this sort of a world that the Dominicans were formally approved as an order in 1216; the Franciscans in 1223. The times urgently needed the friar who could go out of his monastery and combat the evils and errors. Humbert of Romans remarks in his commentary on Dominic's Rule, "Our order has been founded for preaching and for the salvation of our neighbors. Our studies should tend principally, ardently, above everything, to make us useful for souls."[19] St. Francis makes the same point when he records that he felt the most ecstatic joy when he heard the voice of God, "that it behooved him by preaching to convert many people. Thus says the Lord, 'Say to Brother Francis that God has not called him into this estate for himself alone, but to the end that he may gain fruit of souls and that many through him may be saved.' "[20]

This is the essential element in the mendicant transition. Certain aspects of the work of St. Dominic and St. Francis show how this concept was carried out in action. Dominic's order differed from the monastic tradition chiefly in that it had no vow of stability. The Dominicans did not live in isolation, and they maintained a careful, realistic poverty. They devoted themselves to scripture study and to profane science. The Dominican Rule allows a person to be excused from common prayer for the sake of study. This would be quite unthinkable in a strictly monastic tradition.

Even though the Franciscans and Dominicans were founded about the same time and were responding to a similar challenge, the two orders have distinguishing characteristics. Dominic's order was an order of priests from the start; Francis was never a priest. The founding of the Dominicans was altogether unromantic, and it had a very sober and rational attitude from the start. There was much of the romantic tradition in the Italian order of St. Francis. The Dominicans devoted themselves to both religious and secular study, while the earliest Franciscans were not generally interested in intellectual pursuits. The Dominicans turned their attention to the universities of Europe, while the Franciscans engaged themselves more in social and pastoral work.

The Dominicans were a community of canons regular who lived a monastic common life and performed direct apostolic service. Dominic placed great emphasis on organization with a high degree of monastic discipline modified, however, so it could fit in with a vigorous apostolic life.

The Franciscans were part of a voluntary poverty movement that existed at the time. It was also something of a youth movement which flourished in the cities. The movement was directed against the soft secularity of a Christianity that was making itself quite at home in the political and economic world around it.

Within this context the Franciscans quite early in their history experiencd an internal conflict over the interpretation of their poverty. A split developed between the Spirituals, who wanted to follow a very strict poverty, and the Observants who later became known as the Order of Friars Minor. In 1322 the pope condemned the Spirituals, but the split continued. From the Observant branch sprang several new reform movements, the best known of which was the Capuchins.

The number of mendicant friars grew so rapidly that by the early fourteenth century there were fifteen thousand Dominicans and thirty-five thousand Franciscans who together with Augustinians and Carmelites constituted an army of more than eighty thousand mendicants at work throughout Christendom.

More important than the early history of these orders was a theological problem which underlay the whole mendicant movement. The friars were intensely involved in apostolic activity, more so than any other religious group before them had been. And yet they still had the traditions of monasticism deeply inscribed in their religious institutes. The ambiguity we are trying to describe shows up clearly in the life and writing of Thomas à Kempis. *The Imitation of Christ,* a compilation from various sources, reflects the religious thinking of an entire age.

In one place à Kempis tells the reader, "Never be idle or vagrant. Be always reading or writing or praying or meditating, or employed in some useful labor for the common good."[21] This "common good" is no longer restricted to the monastic community, à Kempis and the Brothers of the Common Life were engaged in teaching. But in spite of this, we also find this warning in the *Imitation,* "Fly from the tumult of men as much as you can. We seldom return to silence without prejudice to our conscience. As often as I have been among men, I have returned less a man. It is better to lie hidden and to take care of oneself than to neglect oneself even to work miracles."[22] This theoretical ambivalence between flight and involvement is characteristic of the spirituality of the age and forms its most pressing problem—the need for an understanding and articulation of the spiritual life that does not merely allow for apostolic engagement, but sees that very engagement as a source of holiness.

The ambiguity in à Kempis is also found in Thomas Aquinas. For St. Thomas, the contemplative life, absolutely considered, is better than the active. This thesis reflects the influence of Pseudo-Dionysius and the Origenist spirituality. But later on Thomas says that actually the mixed life is the highest form of life. An apostolic life which is derived from the fullness of contemplation belongs in the realm of the contemplative life, but it rises above pure contemplation insofar as others are given a share in the overflowing fullness of one's own light. "Just as it is better to illuminate than merely to shine, so to pass on what one has contemplated (*contemplata aliis tradere*) is better than merely to contemplate."[23] But we notice here that the active life is appraised from its contemplative element (which is higher) and not from the intrinsic worth of the apostolic work itself. So the problem remains and is heightened through this period of the mendicant transition—can active apostolic work by itself promote union with God; can it be justified on its own intrinsic worth; when the monk leaves his prie-dieu is he necessarily farther from God; is there no theory which will esteem and justify the active life on its own merits alone? Until the sixteenth century no satisfactory answer to these questions would appear.

Religious Climate of the Later Middle Ages

THE FOURTEENTH AND FIFTEENTH CENTURIES were a time of momentous transition and turmoil in western Europe. This was the time of the Black Death, the Hundred Years War, the Avignon Captivity of the popes, and the Great Western Schism with three rival popes trying to rule Christendom. This was also the era of piety represented in *The Imitation of Christ.*

The emphasis we have given the great religious families of Dominic and Francis must be balanced by a more general picture of the religious climate of the times. In his book *The Waning of the Middle Ages,* Johan Huizinga writes:

> To the world when it was half a thousand years younger the outline of all things seemed more clearly marked than they do to us. Life seemed to consist in extremes—a fierce religious asceticism and an unrestrained licentiousness, ferocious judicial punishments and great popular waves of pity and mercy, the most horrible crimes and the most extravagant acts of saintliness—and everywhere a sea of tears. All experience had yet to the minds of men the directness and absoluteness of the pleasure and pain of child life. Every event, every action, was still embodied in expressive and solemn forms which raised them to the dignity of ritual. For it was not merely the great facts of birth, marriage and death which, by the sacredness of the sacraments, were raised to

the rank of mysteries; incidents of less importance, like a journey, a task, a visit, were equally attended by a thousand formalities: benedictions, ceremonies, formulae.[24]

We will try to fill in this picture with an outline of the theories of prayer prevalent at this time and then a description of the popular religious imagination of the same time.

There were basically two different attitudes toward the life of prayer and communion with God around 1300. One attitude developed from the Benedictine tradition and proposed a process of natural development through liturgy and *lectio divina*. This type of prayer is marked by a certain spontaneity, simplicity, and naturalness following the direction of the Holy Spirit. The other type of prayer is scarcely less than a cult of contemplation, a methodical series of psychological techniques for achieving a state of unknowing, a union with God in a very abstruse sense.

This second type of prayer flourished among the Rhineland mystics in the fourteenth century, the great mystic and teacher Meister Eckhart and his three disciples, John Tauler, Blessed Henry Suso, and Blessed Jan van Ruysbroeck. In this second great period of mysticism in the Church (the first being the third and fourth century Eastern monastic period), people again appear who write and talk freely about their mystical experiences.

These Rhineland mystics are basically in the Pseudo-Dionysian tradition and use his vocabulary, the abandonment of all creatures for union with God. Eckhart, for example, says, "One should pray with such energy that he would wish all his limbs, and all his strength, his eyes, ears, mouth, heart, and all his senses were straining within him He should not cease until he seems to have become one with Him who is present and to whom he prays."[25] Eckhart was condemned for "pantheism" because it seemed in his effort to articulate his experience that the self merged into God and was lost.

When trying to understand these mystics, we must realize that it is very difficult for people to express mystical experiences in writing. They were struggling for some way to express what was a genuine gift of God, and human language is quite inadequate to the task. Misunderstanding due to the limitations of language is almost inevitable.

Eckhart explains that when one has achieved a state of union with God, he is in "the abyss without mode and without form of the silent and waste divinity."[26] The fruition of bliss says Ruysbroeck, "is so immense that God himself is as swallowed up with all the blessed in an absence of modes, which is a not-knowing, and in an eternal loss of self."[27] This idea of knowledge of God which is above all knowing is characteristic of this school of mysticism. In the final stage of mystical union, Eckhart teaches, the soul is "buried in the Godhead" and "is God Himself"[28] enjoying all things, disposing all things as God Himself does.

There was another group of mystics who continued the Dionysian and Rhineland tradition in England. There was Richard Rolle, a sort of free-lance hermit who wrote a great deal about the advantages of the contemplative and mystical life (although it seems that he was not a mystic himself). There was Walter Hilton who wrote *The Scale of Perfection* for anchoresses. Another mystic of this period whose name is unknown wrote two books, *The Cloud of Unknowing* and *The Epistle of Privy Counsel.*

There is one English mystic who should be singled out momentarily, for she is an exception to the mystical tradition around her in the fourteenth century. Dame Julian of Norwich wrote only one work, *The Revelations of Divine Love.* Because of its theological depth and great poetic beauty, this work is perhaps the greatest single piece of devotional writing in the English language. Dame Julian's mysticism does not take her into herself, but out to others. She stresses the great wonders of God, a God that acts in history and controls this history, and who will make all things well in the end. Her basic theme is confidence in the divine love as the ultimate reality behind the universe and in the midst of the history of the world.

Up to this point we have concentrated on particular schools of spirituality and on certain religious communities. Now we want to widen the focus and present a brief overview of the spirituality of the people at large in the late Middle Ages, some characteristics of the popular religious imagination of the time.

There was at this time a general all-prevailing desire and attempt to raise all the details of daily life to the level of the sacred and to find religious meaning in the most commonplace activity. We have here one solution to the problem of how to justify action that is not contemplation; it is a practical, not a theoretical solution. There is not an object or an action, however trivial, that is not constantly correlated with Christ and salvation. Bl. Henry Suso, for example, would eat three-quarters of an apple in the name of the Trinity, and the remaining quarter in commemoration of the love with which the heavenly Mother gave her tender child Jesus an apple to eat. And for this reason he eats the last quarter with the paring, as little boys do not peel their apples. After Christmas he does not eat it, for then the infant Jesus was too young to eat apples.[29]

This sounds humorous, but it points out a certain spirit which pervades the popular religious imagination of this period. It is an attempt to superimpose religious significance on all the events in which one is engaged. The effort is psychologically impossible, and it leads neither to a genuine prayer life nor to effective performance of day-to-day activities. Only the schizophrenic could live this theory out perfectly.

There was constant warning by perceptive Church leaders at this time that the Church was being overloaded. A position paper prepared for the Council of Constance in 1414 pointed this out. It showed that with this type of spirituality, the mind eventually gets so flooded with religious images that normal and balanced life is upset. There is too much quantity without quality.

Another problem with this effort is that the legitimately sacred things which should be given reverence get lost in the confusion. The veneration of relics, for example, became mixed with crude primitive ideas and superstitions. The monks at Fossanuova, for instance, for fear of losing the body of Thomas Aquinas, decapitated it, boiled and preserved it.

There was also a great multiplication of saints and saint legends in this period. There was a saint for every conceivable occupation, every town, every house, and literally for everything. There was a saint for preservation from every possible disease and calamity. Masses were multiplied at a great rate; one was developed for every possible title of our Lord and every title of Mary.

The idea of what constituted sanctity gives a further insight into the popular spirituality of the late Middle Ages. If it had been up to the people at large, Blessed Peter of Luxembourg would have been canonized by popular acclaim. He was made bishop of Metz at the age of fifteen and became a cardinal a year later. He carried out a total chastisement of his body denying himself food and every possible convenience. During the last years of his life he always kept his confessor at his side and used to wake up at night in order to go to confession. At his death numerous little slips of paper were found on which Peter had noted down his various faults; he used these in preparation for confession and for meditation on his own unworthiness and sinfulness. He died at the age of eighteen. The cause for his canonization was immediately introduced by no fewer than three kings and the faculty of the University of Paris.

Why did the religious imagination of this period tend to develop such extremes? There was insufficient nourishment for it. Despite the corrective legislation of councils and synods, preaching in general remained relatively poor, except during the first fervor of the friars; vernacular translations of the Bible were often suspect, if not forbidden; and the Mass itself became increasingly distant and unintelligible. The mystics may also have contributed to the problem. Some of the visionaries fed popular imagination and practice with extravagances at best peripheral to the economy of salvation.

It would be dangerous to claim that the people of the later Middle Ages were morally worse or less religious than those of other ages. The evidence actually indicates the opposite—an enormous amount of religious energy. But it was an energy too often unbridled, as sane leaders like Gerson did not cease to warn. Only a few short years later revolution broke out in the Church—a revolution which was in significant measure an attack on the kind of distortions we have been describing.

The Catholic answer to all this was the great Council of Trent. Yet it is legitimate to ask whether this Council was more concerned in some areas with symptoms than with underlying causes. At the level of doctrinal theology, it produced some remarkable decrees; and it succeeded in inaugurating a comprehensive system of moral and doctrinal training for the clergy. But the Council Fathers did not heed legitimate concerns of the Reformers, such as their call for a vernacular liturgy. Thus did the Fathers pass over a basic source of nourishment and a remedy for the unhealthy tendencies of the religious imagination which, some would feel, has remained unreformed even to our own times.

The Nature of Mysticism

ANYONE MORE THAN A LITTLE INTERESTED in the dynamics of spirituality must know something about the nature of mysticism and the theology of it. We will try to present here an outline of the traditional teaching of the theologians on mysticism. Mysticism is not a private phenomenon; it happens in the Church and adds to the richness of the Church's life.

Two crucial elements must be presupposed in any genuine mystical life. One is a certain amount of genuine moral striving towards perfection on the part of the individual. People at enmity with God do not become mystics. Many mystics, of course, were not saints; but there is still a moral orientation towards perfection in the life of anybody involved in genuine mysticism. Secondly, mysticism is a wholly gratuitous gift of God which He gives to whom He pleases.

Mysticism can be defined as the direct and experiential awareness of God's presence in the depths of one's person. This direct awareness of God is unmediated knowledge. In all ordinary human knowledge words, images, concepts and symbols have a necessary and essential function. Not so in mystical experience. Mystical knowledge bypasses these; it is unmediated.

Mystical knowledge also differs from the ordinary

knowledge of faith. By faith one knows that God is present within him, but he is not aware of this experientially. The mystic is somehow actually grasped by God, and he experiences what some mystics struggle to express as tastes and touches of God. Mystics try to indicate something which cannot be described in words and concepts, and so they resort to sense expressions of taste and touch to describe the experience of God.

Finally, mysticism touches the very depths of a person's being. All defenses and facades are totally bypassed. God touches a person where he is most truly himself; and it is at this level that a person knows God as a mystic.

Despite the common denominators we have just pointed out, there is a great diversity in mystics and mysticism, the diversity of many different temperaments reacting to the one great reality that is God. There is theocentric versus Christocentric mysticism, Johannine versus Pauline, Dionysian versus Ignatian; there are historical and environmental factors which influence the various reactions to the experience of God.

The experience of mysticism itself must be carefully distinguished from its possible concomitants: ecstacy, visions, stigmata, levitations and so on.

Visions are traditionally classified into three types: corporeal, imaginative, and intellectual. A corporeal vision is an experience in which a person sees or hears something that is actually physically present outside his imagination. An imaginative vision will seem entirely the same as the corporeal, but it is actually entirely within the imagination. This does not make the imaginative vision any the less genuine. An intellectual vision is an experience of insight or realization with no perceptible sense elements.

Are there corporeal visions? Many have doubts whether there have ever been such visions. Not the least of these are John of the Cross and Theresa of Avila. The impression of reality that a vision seems to have on the visionary is no criterion whether the vision is corporeal or imaginative. A vision of an angel, a pure spirit, must be imaginative. Jesus and Mary have been seen dressed in clothes foreign to the age and culture in which they lived. What is even more significant is the problem of how Christ can now appear bodily as an infant.

The presupposition is in favor of visions being imaginative rather than corporeal. The question of placing these visions within the context of mysticism still remains. The traditional understanding is that visions are not directly caused by God, but are rather an overflow of a more central, purely spiritual process, that of infused contemplation. And so it depends somewhat on a person's temperament whether or not or how the intimate contact with God overflows into a vision.

This context helps to give an understanding of the historical and psychological determinations in visions. It also shows how errors can occur in them. In other words, whatever God causes directly is the intimate mystical union with Himself. He does not directly cause the concomitant experience which may manifest itself in a vision. That experience will be determined partially by the mystical experience of God and partially by the person's own experience and mental makeup.

The case of St. Margaret Mary Alacoque illustrates the historical and psychological determinations in visions. Many have wondered about the origin of the flame above the Sacred Heart, the crown of thorns, and the cross above the heart. Where did they come from? Margaret Mary was a Visitation nun, and all of these symbols were present in the pictorial and devotional traditions of the Visitation order for some time. The mystical experience did not infuse new images and pictures into her mind; they were there and they simply became more clearly focused and more effectively organized as a result of the mystical experience which she had.

The ultimate norm for determining the genuinity of a mystical experience has always been an increase in a person's virtue. By their fruits you shall know them. If God truly establishes a unique union in the depths of a soul, it can only result in a much greater degree of humility and charity in the life of the person. This is the only sure criterion. The great mystics of the Church have always been suspicious of visions and the other concomitant phenomena. History confirms the opinion of a leading theologian that three out of four "visions," even of pious and "normal" people, are pure hallucinations.

Finally there is the question of personal or ecclesial mysticism. Personal visions are those whose object and content solely concern the perfection of the individual himself. Ecclesial or prophetic visions are those which in addition to this induce or commission the visionary to address his environment and ultimately the Church with a message or warning, requiring something, or even on occasion foretelling the future.[30]

The revelations to St. Margaret Mary Alacoque will also illustrate the ecclesial function of mysticism. The Church in the seventeeth century was badly infected with Jansenism. The good news of God's redemptive love for men was clearly contained in the sacred scripture as it always had been, but it was being widely ignored. The purpose and function of the private revelations of the Sacred Heart was simply to recall attention to the fundamental reality of Christ's unfailing love for men. The Sacred Heart devotion did precisely this. The mystical graces granted to St. Margaret Mary were eventually for the good and benefit of the whole Church.

Though our own age and culture are generally unsympathetic to mysticism, yet it is too much a part of the history of the Church to be cast aside. We should have a positive attitude, a respect for genuine mysticism.

But where does one find genuine mysticism? The attitude of the Church has always been one of extreme caution in this regard. Perhaps this should be our attitude too, caution and respect, while at the same time we acknowledge the immense good that has come to the Church from the authentic mystics.

Ignatian Prayer: Finding God in All Things

THE HISTORY OF CHRISTIAN SPIRITUALITY REVEALS a rich variety of forms of prayer, each an effort to achieve union with God. This effort is the common ground of all spiritualities; one only differing from another in its manner or mode of approach to God. One of the most decisive factors determining a spirituality is the prevailing notion of God, who He is, where He is, what He is doing, and accordingly, how He might be approached.

In the Eastern spirituality of Evagrius, Pseudo-Dionysius, and Cassian, the idea of God showed strong Neoplatonic influences: God the supreme transcendent Mind, the pure, immutable One. The approach to God, then, was an effort toward a union of minds, the human with the divine. Contemplation became the ideal of Christian life and perfection. This doctrine has influenced religious thinking, as we have seen, down to our own day.

A more human, simpler, less angelic method of prayer was proposed by Saint Benedict; the chanting of the Divine Office and the quiet, meditative reading of the Sacred Scripture. Both of these forms of prayer require recollection and some withdrawal from other forms of activity. It seems to be at least implicit here that God is thought of chiefly in His transcendence. So the ideal of the Christian life still centers around the periods of formal prayer carried on away from the world in the quiet of the oratory or cell.

The apostolic demand which Pope Gregory I made upon the Benedictines set the conditions for the prayer-action problem which has existed for centuries in the history of spirituality. The problem is a theoretical one, how to justify this activity and work for the neighbor when the ideal of Christian perfection has been identified with a union with God achieved through some form of formal prayer.

The problem is capsulized in Thomas à Kempis. Being among men, he is presumably away from God. The difficulty remained up until the sixteenth century, and no spirituality actually proposed that union with God could be sought and found in the world among men. It first came with Ignatius Loyola.

The revolution in spiritual thinking and practice brought about by St. Ignatius centered around a different idea of God, where He was, what He was doing, and how He might be found. And this led to a radically new kind of prayer and spirituality. With a great mystical grace, Ignatius received a vision of God and the world which could resolve the prayer-action dilemma which we have described above.

The God of Ignatius is He who works the *magnalia Dei* in the world. There is a new, a more biblical emphasis here on God's immanent activity in the world. He continually works the creation of the world; and in the person of Jesus Christ, He works the redemption of men. The God of Ignatius is not deistic or remote. He dwells in creatures and "works and labors for me in all of them."[31]

This notion of God gives rise to a different spirituality. If previous writers conceived of the spiritual life as a union with God in interior prayer, Ignatius, being so taken by God's action in the world, was convinced that a person could achieve a union with God in action just as well as in contemplation. The operative principle then would be a union of will, man's with God's. Ignatius operated on the principle that to find God's will is to find God, and to do God's will, even in total activity, is to be totally united with God. Thus the man of Ignatian spirituality is one who works with God the worker. And this union with God in action Ignatius calls prayer. What he does here is to expand the notion of prayer to include activity; or better, what he does is recommend that a person "find God in all things." The object is a union with God which for Ignatius can be achieved either in prayer, in the traditional sense, or in action by a union of will with God. And so this "finding God in all things" is the epitome of Ignatian prayer and spirituality.

The expression "finding God in all things" is a technical term which embraces several different aspects of the spiritual life. Thus one may find God in formal prayer, in activity by union of will, and one may sometimes find God by an awareness of His presence in the world.

Ignatius never denies the necessity of formal prayer. In fact, the *Spiritual Exercises* are a whole series of meditations, contemplations, and vocal prayers which Ignatius required all of his followers to make. The time of formal prayer could be used for the discernment of spirits, for finding God's will, or for fostering one's sense of the grandeur of God's action in the world, or for simple conversation or presence. Prolonged prayer of this type as a daily practice was always discouraged and generally suspect to Ignatius. That this type of prayer was a means in and not the end of the spiritual life was Ignatius' radical departure from the contemplation ideal of other spiritualities.

A second aspect of "finding God in all things" is the Ignatian prayer of direct action based upon a union of will. "We have a formula in Ignatian prayer, *in actione contemplativa,* wholly different from the *contemplata tradere* of St. Thomas. Casting off the last vestiges of the Neo-Platonic techniques, Igantius affirms that the Christian mystical union is essentially the union of love where correspondence to the divine will is more important than psychological techniques and which can therefore be acquired no matter what the circumstances."[32]

According to this kind of prayer, it is sufficient to seek to discover God's will and then to carry it out vigorously with full attention on the work to be done with no concomitant vision or contemplation. "In activity and in study, . . . when we direct everything to the service of God, everything is prayer."[33] We can see here that Ignatius had an enriched and broader notion of prayer. For him "the word prayer means now a disinterested prayer which is established in the solitude of the heart and then the spiritual attitude which causes us to 'find God' in the midst of activity, even the most absorbing. On the one hand, prayer is considered as a particular and definite 'exercise' and, on the other, the continuous union with God in activity."[34]

It is because a union of will in action is his primary approach to union with God that Ignatius puts so much stress on obedience and a right intention in all things. The Discernment of Spirits is one way to discover the will of God.

This union of will with God must not be thought of as mechanical or military. For Ignatius the motive force and the essence of this union was always a personal love of God.

While reserving a place for formal prayer, Ignatius always preferred the prayer of action, collaboration with God in the great deeds which He does in the world. This makes for an action-oriented spirituality of total service for the kingdom of Christ. It is a spirituality which provides a theoretical support for apostolic work, and it explains how one who engages himself fully in the work is no farther from God than the contemplative at his prie-dieu. He may be closer.

In the writings of St. Ignatius the formula "finding God in all things" is used in still another sense to describe a certain perceptual awareness of the presence of God in the world which he experienced daily and which in some analogous form he recommended to his followers. Jerome Nadal wrote of Ignatius that "in all things, actions, conversations, he felt and contemplated the presence of God and the attraction of spiritual things. He was a contemplative in action, something he expressed habitually in the words: we must find God in all things."[35] This peculiar prayer was the result of mystical graces of a very high order. Ignatius is ranked with the greatest mystics in the history of the Church.

Despite the gratuity of Ignatius' own gifts, we find that he used the same formula to 'to find God in all things' to recommend a form of prayer for Jesuit scholastics who had not been in the Society for a long time and certainly were not expected to have had the mystical graces which he had. They were advised to seek God in all things.

> Considering the end of study, the scholastics can hardly give themselves to prolonged meditation. Over and above the spiritual exercises assigned for their perfection, namely daily Mass, an hour for vocal prayer and examen of conscience, weekly confession and communion, they should exercise themselves in seeking our Lord's presence in all things, in their conversation, their walks, in what they see, taste, hear, understand, and in everything they do, since it is clear that His divine majesty is in all things by his presence, power, and essence. And this kind of meditation which finds God our Lord in all things is easier than raising oneself to the consideration of divine truths which are more abstract and demand more of an effort if we are to keep our attention on them.[36]

Ignatius here recommends a simpler kind of prayer which focuses upon the omnipresence of God with special emphasis upon His immanence in things, persons, situations, and experiences. If Nadal's phrase, "contemplation in action" is used, the contemplation idea must be purged of all Neo-Platonic overtones which suggest an interior exercise carried on in solitude and silence. It is rather a wide-awake, eyes-open sort of thing that seeks to find God who is present and active in the world, in history, in the activities of men. In the midst of activity, the apostle may sense that what he is doing is God's work, that God is present and active in him and in the situation. It is some sort of an on-going sense or awareness that God is active here. Jean Danielou says that the Ignatian man

> ought to be a saint and he ought to live in complete activity. Previous spirituality opposed these two aspects. Activity seemed to be an obstacle to holiness which was conceived as contemplation. The revolution accomplished by St. Ignatius showed that that which appeared to be an obstacle could become a means. To the heart filled with God, all things speak of Him. And it is not a question merely of an orientation of the will, but of a spiritual experience where God is 'tasted' in everything.[37]

The language of sense experience keeps recurring in the description of this kind of prayer, and along with it the indication that there are many different degrees of this finding God in all things. At one end there is the basic union of will with the simple conviction and satisfaction that "I am doing what God wants me to do." At the other extreme is great mystical experience, a constant awareness of the presence of God in all things, the highest perfection of the virtue of faith.

> It would be imprudent to believe that one could go very quickly to God through creatures . . . St. Francis of Assisi chanted the Canticle of the Sun, but only after having been the stigmatist of Alverno. What St. Ignatius describes to us then is an idea of consummated perfection, of a soul so totally filled with God that everything leads to God. Thus, the spiritual itinerary takes place completely between the moment when creatures are obstacles and the moment they become means. The *Contemplatio ad Amorem* . . . describes for us the state of a man who has arrived at this perfection. According to the words of St. Ignatius, "He loves God in all creatures and all creatures in God."[38]

Contemplative Climate
in 16th-Century Spain

IN EVERY AGE OF THE CHURCH God reveals Himself to men in the Sacred Scriptures, but not every age has always seen the message clearly and in proper perspective. To correct this vision can be one of the functions of the ecclesial mystic. Under God's direction he discerns something in the scripture which a whole age may have failed to perceive. It seems that few people in sixteenth-century Spain found God as Ignatius Loyola did. The religious climate with its contemplative ideal was quite contrary to that of Ignatius Loyola.

The cultural and religious climates of sixteenth-century Spain interacted on each other and had a profound influence on the western world. We will try to indicate just what that atmosphere was.

Spain was the great power of the sixteenth-century. She had just successfully concluded an eight hundred year struggle to drive the Moors out of her land. The people were basking in the glory of this final triumph. They had the finest army and navy in the world; and up to half of Europe—the Austrian Empire, the Low countries, and much of Italy—was under Spanish control. But more than all of this, the fact that Spain was pure Catholic made the Spaniards raise their heads in pride. Spain was untainted by the terrible Protestant Reformation, and this was her greatest glory.

Sixteenth-century Spain witnessed a full flowering of the baroque spirit which was epitomized in the royal palace of Philip II, the Escorial. This huge complex of palace, fortress, library, and church was built around 1560 as a monument to the Catholic victory over the Moors.

The Escorial, a contemporary historian has written, is no mere monument of victory, no triumphal arch, but a confession of Catholicity born of the Spanish soul. Here according to the chronicler we see the king's longing for unity, for he did not want to rule over heretics. The architecture aims at the expression of spiritual things, God is the intended goal. Eight hours a day are devoted to the Eucharistic liturgy and the Divine Office in the church. The adoration of the Blessed Sacrament must be continuous, and no fewer than one hundred monks are constantly employed in this task. There was also a great library, for God must be served here too in study and scholarship. But in the midst of all this splendor and greatness we find the king himself living as a simple monk in an austere apartment, the most humble of the servants of the Lord.[39] We see here greatness of soul together with religious devotion, penance, and renunciation.

We must turn now to the contemplative ideal of this age if we are to understand the religious spirit which was at its heart. A reputable historian of the period claims that there were no fewer than three thousand writers on the contemplative life and mysticism in sixteenth-century Spain. This indicates how powerfully the mystical ideal had captivated the religious imagination of the age. If one wished to be a perfect Christian, he would have to go to a monastery and become a contemplative monk or nun.

This identification of the contemplative life and Christian perfection gained great impetus from the writings of two great mystics of the period, John of the Cross and Theresa of Avila. Because these people wrote about their own deep mystical experiences, they influenced others and the popular religious imagination. Many wanted to have the same kind of experiences and to find the same intimate touch of God in mystical union. This was the perfection of the Christian life.

Along with the glories of sixteenth-century Spanish mysticism, there were also dangers, delusions, and excesses, particularly in a kind of latent heresy called illuminism. Those identified with the movement are known as the Alumbrados or Illuminati. They claimed to have reached such a height of mystical union with God that it was no longer necessary for them to pay any attention to any authority, even the hierarchical church. If one had this direct contact with God in mystical experience, it was no longer believed possible to commit sin or to be mistaken in one's religious ideas.

But the Inquisition was also at the height of its power in Spain at this time, and it did not take long for it to catch up with the Alumbrados. Many of them were questioned and imprisoned. The Inquisition with its peculiarly successful methods did much to stamp out this Alumbrado movement.

From all this we can move back to the question of the effect of this climate on the Society of Jesus. At the death of Ignatius Loyola in 1556, more than half, perhaps almost two-thirds, of all Jesuits came from this Spain which we have been describing—this Spain which had such a tremendous longing for mystical union with God, for flight from the world, for identifying Christian perfection with the contemplative life. In view of these facts, then, we simply raise the question, how could the Society of Jesus after the death of Ignatius fail to be effected by the religious currents we have described.

Jesuit Prayer

Second Generation

WITHIN THE CONTEXT OF SIXTEENTH-CENTURY PIETY, we have noted that Ignatian spirituality is characterized by an interior disposition of soul by which one's union with God is centered about whole-hearted action for the greater glory of God and the Kingdom of Christ. The interior aspect of union of wills is exteriorly manifested by tireless, loving service of the Church, whatever her immediate needs may be. In Ignatius' vision it is precisely this ceaseless and unselfish labor that detaches the apostle from himself and centers him more and more on Christ, and so the work becomes an exercise of prayer and union with God.

Now this orientation towards apostolic labor produces a challenge of its own. Ignatius' emphasis on action might be taken as a de-emphasis on formal prayer. Ignatius held that both prayer and action done according to God's will are basically two aspects of the same thing, the love of God. But while this was clear to Ignatius himself, one might ask how he expressed this in the Constitutions of the Society and how the fathers who followed him interpreted and altered this Constitution.

In the Constitutions of the Society of Jesus, Ignatius prescribed that every applicant to the order make the thirty-day Spiritual Exercises. This would culminate in a personal conversion and commitment. The exercitant was educated in a school of prayer and became a "mortified" man, not one who fasted twenty-four hours, but one who was oriented toward God and saw Him above everything else.

But the mental prayer of the Exercises was not to be a permanent or universal form of prayer for all followers. It was rather a point of departure. For Ignatius, prayer was a style of life, something organic that grows under its own power and the guidance of the Holy Spirit, something which issues in a life of prayerful action.

The Constitutions of the Society, approved in 1558, did outline a certain varied and flexible program of spiritual exercises; but no single program was obligatory on all. For scholastics, the program called for weekly communion and confession, and daily Mass, plus one hour of prayer which was to include the two examens, the office of the Blessed Virgin, and other prayers of their liking. All this was to be under the direction of the spiritual father.

For those fathers who had been admitted to final vows in the Society, "it must be taken for certain that they will be spiritual men . . . so progressed in the way of Christ our Lord that they can run in it as much as their care for health and external works of charity and obedience will allow . . . . For chastisement of the body it does not seem necessary that any regulation be written down except that mature charity will dictate whatever is necessary for each one. Nevertheless, let each one's confessor always be consulted and whenever any question comes up about what should be done, let the matter be brought to the superior."[40] Thus mature charity under direction is the universal principle.

These were essential elements of the Constitution and Ignatius would never consider changing any one of them in the least. He said explicitly that it was "his opinion from which no one would ever move him that for those who are studying, one hour of prayer was sufficient, it being supposed they are practicing mortification and self denial."[41]

When Jerome Nadal visited the Spanish provinces (1553-54) and yielded to their request for one and a half hours of daily prayer, Ignatius was angered and according to Nadal's own account "thereafter he did not make great use of my services."[42]

With these notions from the Ignatian Constitutions in mind, we can now consider the changes that occurred in the Society's practice of prayer and the factors which brought them about. We have seen that Ignatius stood on the side of freedom and flexibility. The prayer life was to be determined under the guidance of the Holy Spirit and the spiritual director. Prayer must be shaped to meet personal needs and abilities. Now this sort of attitude is not peculiar to Ignatius; it is true of many great founders of religious communities. But pressures soon arise as institutions expand which tend to program performance in order to secure and insure certain ideals of the organization. This is just what happened with Jesuit prayer in the second generation.

Internal pressures soon arose. Spanish and Portuguese superiors feared a tepidity was creeping into the Society in matters of humility and obedience and they wanted regulations set up regarding prayer. To bolster the humility, obedience, and loss of spirit especially in the younger men, these superiors attempted to solve the difficulty by prescribing a certain amount of time for formal prayer. This was consonant, of course, with the contemplative context in which they were living. Reform movements also have a way of programming things in order to insure their objectives. For example, Francis Borgia, the third general of the Society of Jesus, lived in the Spanish community of Gandia under Andreas Ovieto. In this particular house the fathers and scholastics were accustomed to spend three hours a day in prayer and meditation. The wonder is that when Borgia became general he only introduced one hour of prescribed meditation and not more!

The rapid numerical increase of members in the Society was another factor which tended to dilute the original fervor and spirit and seemed to call for some sort of remedial action.

The non-Jesuit contemplative tradition, especially in Spain, created another pressure for an increased amount of obligatory prayer for all. Ignatius withstood this environmental pressure; his followers apparently could not.

All of these pressures for a prescribed amount of obligatory prayer came to bear on the early Society. Jesuits in northern Europe, France, Holland, and Germany resisted any change in the Constitutions. Those in southern Europe, the majority, chiefly from Spain and Italy, argued for a change.

The Second General Congregation in 1565 elected Francis Borgia general, and after a split of opinion left the matter of increased prescribed prayer up to him to decide. One month after the congregation closed Borgia prescribed the full hour of prayer for all members of the Society.

Some other developments came in at this same time. In 1566 Pope Pius V asked the Society if they would say some litanies for the resolution of the Turkish problem in eastern Europe. Thus a temporary request became prescribed, institutionalized, and the litanies have been said regularly until just recently. Visits after meals, begun as a pious custom, eventually became almost a rule of architectural design so that one could hardly avoid making a visit after meals on his way to recreation. Rosaries came to be worn with cassocks because Father Borgia wore one. In 1572 prescribed spiritual reading was introduced.

By the time of the Third Congregation (1573) a considerable movement had developed within the Society to return to the original spirit and letter of the Constitutions of St. Ignatius in the matter of prayer. A number of provincial superiors made the request, but Father General Mecurian simply refused to yield on the practice of Father Borgia.

"Nihil innovandum est." No innovation was to be made on Borgia's innovation! But dispensations were allowed for the weak and for foreseeable conflicts.

But the practice of obligatory prayer introduced a new problem which appears most pointedly in a letter written to the general in 1576 by the French provincial, Father Claude Matheieu.

> Will your paternity please consider whether in the Society it is fitting that the period of time for prayer be observed which is prescribed in the Constitutions, and that the increase of prayer be removed which was introduced some years ago. For I notice that Ours are less fervent in prayer now than previously. Indeed in the past they often used to ask permission to give more time to prayer, and perhaps they spent more time then on prayer than they do now . . . . But nowadays many ask to be dispensed from the increase in prayer. Thus in a very short time there will be more people who are dispensed, or what is worse, more people who will dispense themselves, than those who, as is now the case, observe the rule. It has always seemed to me that we will accomplish not a little if we simply and perfectly observe those things which are in our Constitutions, because if we wish to adopt other things, there is fear that little by little the practice of what is prescribed in our Constitutions will cease, and finally we will learn to our discomfort that it would have been better if we had remained in the simplicity of our fathers.[43]

What was initiated by Father Borgia in this matter of a legislated amount of daily prayer was maintained by Father Mecurian and was solidly confirmed and entrenched by Father Aquaviva who was general from 1581 to 1615.

How can we interpret this development in the matter of prayer? It seems to be a normal and legitimate instance of institutionalization, a result of the effort to organize and stabilize a religious way of life. There can be no real objection to this. But a definite difficulty arises when one particular form of the development becomes "consecrated" so to speak, institutionalized, and irreversible for subsequent generations. Times and cultures change, and what may have been a suitable embodiment of the Ignatian ideal in Francis Borgia's time (though this is open to question too), may not be at all suitable in another culture centuries later, and may not be suitable in our own time.

The development from Ignatius to Aquaviva is something like the development from apostolic Christianity of the first century to the established Catholicism of the fourth and fifth. What happened was a routinization of religious life. The greatest danger here is not the change, but that a particular form of change should become inflexible and irreversible. Some regularization of religious spirit will be inevitable in a large religious community, but it should be constantly adaptable and adapted to various times and circumstances.

And then perhaps Ignatius' original working principle concerning prayer would still be the best of all· prayer as a style of life, a seeking to find God in all things, with formal prayer as a means of disposing the individual to do God's will, the time to be determined by mature charity under the guidance of the Holy Spirit and the spiritual father.

On the evidence presented we can speak of a real distinction between Ignatian prayer and Jesuit prayer. But as we read the history of the past and question the legislation of another age, we must still discern and determine how best to adapt the spirit and ideal of a founder to the circumstances of our own time.

Finding God's Will:
Discernment

IN HIS BOOK CALLED *The Love of God,* Dom Aelred Graham talks about the distinctive virtues of some of the great saints in the history of the Church. The virtue most revealed in the life of St. Benedict, he says, was religion. In the life of St. Thomas Aquinas, faith joined with wisdom. In St. Ignatius, he suggests, the virtue is supernatural prudence and discernment. We might note in passing that this virtue of Ignatius is one of the most misunderstood elements of his spirituality.

Ignatius Loyola learned the art of discernment through his efforts to interpret the profound spiritual experiences he had at the time of his conversion. We find the principles of this discernment described in the book of the Spiritual Exercises. Ignatius considered the art of discernment a *sine qua non* of the Exercises and in a certain sense the whole purpose of a retreat—to learn how to discover the will of God, most especially how to choose among various alternative good possibilities of action.

But where is God's will? Which means will be most conducive to the honor and glory, the service and love of God? It is precisely at this point that the Rules for the Discernment of Spirits apply. These rules are essential to Ignatian spirituality, but they also transcend it and are universally applicable in any Christian tradition.

At the outset it is important to note that for Ignatius there is no question whatever of choices for God's glory coming as a result of human initiative or ascetic discipline. Any human effort in this direction is initiated by the grace of Christ through the action of the Holy Spirit. So also the enemy of the Church and of human nature is spiritual and personal, Satan. In this context, in a spiritual conflict, good and evil spirits are polarized and the primary battleground is the heart of man. From patristic and medieval tradition Ignatius took the idea that God, angels, and demons more or less regularly invade human consciousness producing virtuous or sinful inclinations. To identify the source of these impulses, discernment is needed. We may not look on spirits in precisely this way, but the underlying reality is valid enough: powers of good and evil experienced as a kind of personal and powerful force taking hold of people as well as the general atmosphere.[44]

There are two different levels of discernment, and St. Ignatius divides them into two sets of rules. The first set goes with the First Week of the Spiritual Exercises, and the second set with the following weeks. The First Week has a distinctive purpose, to prepare a person to receive the grace of God by taking some fundamental considerations about themselves and the world around them. One tries to locate oneself in the world, in relationship to God, and to see where they stand, and to assess their value system. Once this is done and the need for contact with God is realized, a person can then confront the distinctly Christian vocation of following Christ. Once a person realizes that God is an operative force in their life, they start to ask themselves how they can serve God better. The problem of sin is transcended and they move toward the goal of a closer following of Christ.

We see, then, that there are two phases, choosing between good and evil (First Week, Rules I), and then the choice among various alternative goods, how to follow

Christ more closely (Second Week, Rules II). When the choice is no longer between good and evil, but among various goods, things can become confused, and a person wonders how they can know that a particular way of behaving or a particular choice is God's will or not. This is where discernment comes in.

The two basic states of soul, the matter for discernment, Ignatius calls consolation and desolation. Consolation is the complete love of God with an increase of faith, hope, and charity, and interior joy. Desolation is the opposite, darkness of soul, turmoil of spirit, restlessness, temptations against faith, hope, and love.

For a person going from one mortal sin to another, the evil spirit presents apparent pleasures, sensual delights, and gratifications; for the same person the good spirit causes remorse and the sting of conscience.

For one moving from sin to love of God, the spirits act the very opposite: the evil one harasses with anxiety, sadness, and obstacles; the good spirit gives courage, strength, consolation, and peace.

So at the beginning a person must know the basic orientation of their life and then develop a keen sensitivity about how they feel. When one is experiencing desolation, Ignatius advises that they be patient, realize that God has left them on their own, and be assured that God will give sufficient grace to overcome that state of soul. When one is in consolation, they should store up strength against desolation and humbly recognize the source of their well-being.

Ignatius then exposes three tactical maneuvers of the enemy. 1) He conducts himself like a woman, weak in face of strong resistance to temptation, and a tyrant if he has the upper hand. 2) He also acts like a false lover who seeks to remain hidden and wants his proposals and actions kept secret. If his seductions and temptations are revealed to a confessor or another person, he knows he cannot succeed. 3) The enemy is like a military commander who attacks a stronghold at its weakest point, so he will assault a person with temptations where their virtue is weakest.

Now these Rules for the First Week are fairly straight-forward. One is just becoming sensitive to experiences in the spiritual life; the basic choice is between sin and non-sin, and the lines are fairly clearly drawn between good and evil. But people advance in the spiritual life and their decisions become somewhat more subtle; the choices are then among alternative goods.

In the Rules for the Second Week the presuppositions are rather different. They suppose that there are definite movements, feelings, impulses, determinisms going on in the soul, and that the person is sensitive to them. The choice is now among alternative good courses of action, this or that way of life, this or that mission where the choice is open and all the possibilities are good. Then the distinctions between the various choices are not too clear, but complex and some-times confused.

An example from Jean Paul Sartre's book *Existentialism as a Humanism* illustrates the situation of a person trying to discover the greater good. A pupil of his during the Nazi occupation was anxious to decide whether he ought to leave home and join the Free French forces, or stay at home and help his mother who was sick and very much dependent on him. There were two alternatives, both good, and the young man was torn between the demands of filial devotion and patriotic generosity. No one could settle the problem for him; in the last analysis the student himself would be re-sponsible for his own choice. In advising him Satre goes on to say, "I had but one reply to make; You are free, therefore choose. That is to say, invent. No rule of general morality can show you what you ought to do. No signs are given in this world. We ourselves decide our being . . . . Decide your future, you alone are responsible for it."[45]

Here is a situation in which the general rules of moral-ity do not provide a solution for a particular problem. It is not that in such a case it is difficult to decide what is right, but that it is simply impossible by Christian reason alone to know God's will precisely here and now. Another method must be sought. Ignatius proposes that it lies in the discernment of spirits. It is the method he describes in the Second Time of Choosing a State of Life, "when much light and understanding are derived through experience of desolations and consolations and discernment of diverse spirits."[46]

The focus of our attention here, Ignatius would insist, is not voluntary will acts or choices, but involuntary movements or determinisms, the things that happen to us no matter what we may want. We feel consolation or not, desolation or not, and there is nothing we can do about it. But Ignatius urges that we pay close attention to these determinisms because it is in them that the good and evil spirits are at work, and through them that we can discern the will of God.

The consolation which is peculiarly indicative is that which comes to the soul "without any previous cause."[47] This is given by God alone. No perceivable cause or object produces it; it is self-validating. This consolation is felt as a conscious experience of grace, of the love of God, in which the soul is drawn "wholly to the love of His Divine Majesty."[48]

Ignatius says this consolation may occur in the context of a choice of a way of life, so that as one considers one alternative, they may experience peace, joy, tranquility, enthusiasm, or simply openness to God. The right decision leaves the consolation of the union with God intact. This is the spirit of God confirming a person in this particular choice. There is a certain congruousness, propriety, rightness in this course of action; it is in line, on target, tending toward the service and glory of God. There is a goodness about it; it contributes to a closer union with God. In a letter to Theresa Rajadell in 1536, Ignatius wrote about this particular point:"It remains for me to speak how we ought to understand what we think is from the Lord, and, understanding it, how we ought to use it for our advantage. For it frequently happens that Our Lord moves and urges the soul to this or that activity. He begins by enlightening the soul; that is to say, by speaking interiorly to it without the din of words, without any possibility of resistance on our part, even should we wish to resist."[49] Ignatius seems to be describing here what he calls consolation without a cause.

But in contrast to this consolation without any perceptible cause, Ignatius describes the possibility of consolation when a known cause precedes, such as good or pious thoughts; and this consolation can come from either the good or evil spirit. In order to discern the spirit in this circumstance he advises a person to review the whole course of their thoughts; if they begin good and end in something evil, distracting, or less good, they are the work of the evil spirit who began by assuming the appearance of goodness. The judgment here, where causes can be identified, is something of an application of the principle, by their fruits you shall know them. Where no cause is discernible, the consolation must be from God.

Before we leave this matter of how to discover the will of God in a particular concrete choice, it will be important to consider certain recent theological thinking about the will of God itself. Is the will of God a pre-arranged plan in the divine mind (let us say B), so that as I choose among alternate goods A, B, and C, if I choose A, I might actually be missing the will of God for me? Or is the crucial part of finding God's will in the process itself and not in the thing chosen? Could finding God's will be not so much choosing the right object but simply in choosing for God? So that the will of God will coincide with whatever alternative good I choose providing I am truly seeking God and not simply myself in the choosing?

As we move away from a static, structured view of the world and ourselves and begin to see things in process and evolution, we are getting away from the notion that there may be some eternal blueprint in the mind of God which we might discover if we follow the right procedure. There is really no will of God in this sense. God's will for the world and for people is bound up with His creative act, His divine knowledge and support of the creative processes in the world and particularly in the creativity of man. "It is in this context that human decision-making is really, if you want, the process of determining the will of God. This is what God is doing—He is sustaining creatively this process by which human beings, with several options before them, and in many cases options which are relatively neutral, any one of which might be a good choice—they are the cutting-edge of what you might call the Will of God. That is why we are here. We human beings are meant to shape the development of history and the development of evolution, even of the cosmos itself, from this point onward."[50]

This magnificent realization of man's co-creativity with God in the making of the future is a product of our own age. We cannot say that Ignatius had this view of the world and of God's will, but we can say that his method for decision-making based on the discernment of spirits is congruent and compatible with this view. For as a person ponders or considers a certain good course of action (A), they will experience that consolation, which God alone gives, that peace, joy, felt-compatibility, that rightness of choice, only if they are truly choosing for God. And then whatever the particular concrete choice they make in this context, it can be said to be the will of God no matter what its specific content may be. What Ignatius proposes is a methodology for choosing which places the emphasis not on the concrete particularities of the choices but on the conditions and context out of which the choice is made. Once again, what is chosen is not so important as that the choice be made in faith, in grace, in love, and for the service of God. It is the dispositions, the intentions, and the motives that are most important. These were Ignatius' primary concerns.

Spirituality for Our Time

ARE THE ESSENTIAL ELEMENTS of traditional spirituality viable in an active apostolic life today? Can we find a solid spirituality operative in the life of a person who is deeply attuned to our own times? We can find just this in the life and writings of Pierre Teilhard de Chardin, S.J. His world view is at once contemporary and profoundly spiritual; contemporary because evolutionary, he sees the world in process; and spiritual because his is a faith-vision of the world and of man.

Teilhard de Chardin was a French Jesuit priest and a world-renowned paleontologist. Since his death in 1955 his writings have been published and many of them have been translated into English. Teilhard has profoundly influenced our time and has caught the fancy of hundreds of thousands of people, believers and non-believers alike. The purpose of this chapter will be to sketch in barest outline Teilhard's faith-vision of the world, and then to describe his spirituality, a finding God in all things, which follows upon this vision.

The fundamental premise in Teilhard's vision is that the world is in process; it is in a state of becoming; it is in evolution. "To our clearer vision the universe is no longer a State but a Process. The cosmos has become a Cosmogenesis."[51] Cosmogenesis is Teilhard's own term for the ordered whole of the world in the process of becoming. The world is developing, moving from the stages of pre-life, to life, toward the perfection of human thought and knowledge and unanimity. This changed notion of the world, from smething static to something in process, is fundamental for the understanding of our times.

In his major work, *The Phenomenon of Man,* Teilhard begins with the phenomenon of biology, and this for him reveals biogenesis; namely, that in the world of living things there is an emerging process, a biological development which advances towards consciousness and then the rise of consciousness. Teilhard sees a line of progress developing towards consciousness, the power of a living thing to know, to sense, and to be aware of the world around it. This rise of increasing consciousness marks the axis of evolution. As biogenesis develops, it reaches a point where reflex consciousness appears, and this is man.

There are two dynamic principles in this process of evolution as Teilhard observed it: complexification and convergence. Complexification is quite simply the ordered numerical multiplication of units, more and more molecules, cells, or whatever units may be in question. This is a principle of and a key to progress. Quite simply Teilhard observes as a biologist the more cells the higher degree of consciousness. Psychic energy increases with the complexity of organized units. The second principle is that of convergence, the gathering of elements or units together into an organized and unified pattern. This is not only multiplication of units, but also their coming together and interacting with each other.

The phenomenon of man begins at the threshold of reflection. When consciousness becomes self-consciousness, when biogenesis develops to the point where consciousness reflects upon itself, the phenomenon of man appears. Man not only knows, but knows that he knows. With the emergence of man, of reflex consciousness in the world, a new kind of growth appears, that of human knowledge and personality. The world is enveloped, as it were, with another sphere, another layer of life, the noosphere, the sphere of knowledge, the growth of science. This growth and development of science Teilhard calls noogenesis from the Greek word *nous*, mind, and genesis, the process of becoming. Noogenesis describes the evolution of man, his growth in consciousness and knowledge.

The principles which foster human growth and development (hominization) are the same ones which Teilhard discovered operating in biological evolution: complexity and convergence. Complexification, here more and more human beings, more centers of consciousness, quite simply the increasing world population, Teilhard sees as contributing to human development. Convergence: the physical and psychic interaction of people, communication, socialization. The very roundness of the world itself guarantees and contributes to this convergence of persons.

Although people will multiply and increase regularly, their social convergence is not fully guaranteed. There are counter-dynamics which jeopardize the process of human unification toward unanimity; they are selfishness, isolationism, divisiveness, egocentricity, war, and in the Christian context, sin. Human freedom creates these possibilities which endanger the whole evolutionary process and render its ultimate success doubtful and insecure.

What then is the human ultimate? Teilhard calls this the Omega point. He takes his basic vision and projects it into the future. He sees a supreme act of collective vision. There are indications of this development in our world today; the scientific explosion and the great increase of knowledge tend towards this supreme act of collective vision. He then projects his vision of human convergence to what he terms a megasynthesis, a great synthesis of all human beings. This socialization is gradually taking place, for instance, in a metropolis where many people come together and interact. In a sense the city is the spearhead of evolution and progress, the center of modern life.

Teilhard's appendix to *The Phenomenon of Man* is called "The Christian Phenomenon" and here he turns from scientific data and hypothetical projection to the data of Christian revelation. Here the end of all process and all evolution is already given. Omega already exists and is operative at the core of all being. Teilhard says it radiates from one center to all centers personally. In other words, the whole dynamic evolution of the world is the result of the attractive force of the Omega point who is God Himself supporting, energizing, and working in this whole process. He is present and working in the world according to the principles of complexification and convergence.

Teilhard finds the presence of God in the world and throughout the world. He develops this aspect of his vision in his book *The Divine Milieu.* Here is a profoundly faith-oriented vision of the world and of God the Alpha and Omega of all creation. God created the world, or better, creates the world; for Teilhard's notion of creation is not the making of a static world, but that of continuous creation in which God works constantly through complexification and convergence to bring the world ever closer to perfection and to Himself.

The creation of the cosmos, an ongoing process, is for Teilhard a progressive cosmogenesis, biogenesis, noogenesis, and ultimately Christogenesis, in which each process prepares for and leads to and supports the next one. And because God supports and works throughout the whole series, He is everywhere, omnipresent, a divine milieu.

Teilhard finds God at the very source of human life and the source of all that happens to people in the world. God is present in all that influences a person both from within and without.

Teilhard even finds God working in the diminishments

of suffering and of death: ". . . when I feel I am losing hold of myself and am absolutely passive within the hands of the great unknown forces that have formed me, in all these dark moments, O God, grant that I may understand that it is You, provided only my faith is strong enough, who are painfully parting the fibers of my being in order to penetrate to the very marrow of my substance and bear me away within yourself."[52]

But the crowning instance of the presence of God in the world is the Incarnation of Jesus Christ. In him God enters the world in a special, historical way and assumes dynamic leadership of all of cosmic evolution. Teilhard's notion of redemption is one which follows to a great extent the principles of biological evolution and development. At the divine inbreak of Christ, God immerses Himself and identifies Himself with the whole process of evolution. He ultimately redeems people and the world by uniting them to Himself organically in Christ Jesus. In the Pauline sense people are redeemed by a physical incorporation into the Body of Christ. It is then through Him and with Him and in Him that all are returned to the Father.

The process of redemption in Christ Jesus is also a process of unification of people, the ultimate instance of convergence of people in love. It is Christ who by His life and by His grace energizes this same dynamic of convergence and guarantees its ultimate success and perfection.

The chief instrument through which Christ energizes, amorizes, and unifies the faithful within Himself is the Eucharist. Teilhard's notion of the Eucharist is not simply that it is formed and communicated to persons, but that it pervades and permeates those who receive it and through them it comes into contact with the whole material world. This is the expansion of the Host which penetrates the whole of creation. But then from this extension, from this permeation of the hearts of people and of the world, Christ draws all to Himself. ". . . Christ Jesus, who through the magnetism of his love and the effective power of his Eucharist, gradually gathers into himself all the unitive energy scattered through his creation."[53] With St. Paul, Teilhard would say to the Christians, "All things are yours, and you are Christ's, and Christ is God's."

What will the consummation of this process be? What will the second coming of Christ be all about? Teilhard poses the question whether the world has two summits of fulfillment, or only one. In other words, does the world have a natural end and a supernatural end too? His answer is no; "the world can no more have two summits of fulfillment than a circumference can have two centers."[54] To build the earth is to prepare for and to hasten the second coming of Christ. This then verifies Teilhard's notion that what Christ has done by his Incarnation is to enter this whole dynamic of the human world and to lead the whole process to His heavenly Father where God will be all in all. All the processes within the world will be assumed by Christ and led to the Father. Teilhard writes, "in a universe which was disclosing itself to me as structurally convergent, you, Lord Jesus, by right of your resurrection had assumed the dominating position of all-inclusive Center in which everything is gathered together."[55]

So Teilhard sees the evolving universe centered, focused into a single redeeming and elevating process. All things will be united to Christ and find their fulfillment in Him. There will be a new heaven and a new earth when Christ reestablishes all things in Himself and finally returns all to his Father.

This has been a sketch of Teilhard's faith-vision of God, people, and the world. It is the basis for his Ignation spirituality of finding God in all things.

To capsulize the implications of this booklet, we might distinguish four aspects of the spiritual life which may well be components for an apostolic Christian life in our time.

The first aspect is a Christian outlook; this is a reflex, intellectual faith-vision of the world. This is the way a person sees things, the way they interpret their experience. In moments of reflection or writing or serious conversation a person may articulate their vision of the world. What we have just seen above is an epitome of Teilhard's vision of the world. For a Christian this vision will be a faith-vision. The way a person understands God, people, and the world will have a profound influence on their whole spirituality.

The second aspect of any spirituality must be a finding or seeking God in formal prayer. This is raising the heart and mind to God in meditation, contemplation, and liturgical prayer. It is an interior exercise of prayer which we saw for Ignatius was not an end, but a means in the spiritual life. It can be used to foster and enrich one's faith-vision; it may be a means for finding God's will, a time for discernment; and it is ordered to the service of God and action for the kingdom of Christ. We meet this sort of prayer in the Spiritual Exercises of Ignatius. We also find this type of prayerful expression throughout the writings of Teilhard. "But for these moments of more efficient or more explicit contact, the tide of the divine omnipresence and our perception of it would weaken until all that was best in our human endeavor, without being entirely lost to the world, would be emptied of God."[56]

A third aspect of the spiritual life is finding God in activity. This is prayer as a style of life in God's service. To find God's will is to find God, and to do God's will is to be united with God. Teilhard writes, "let us ponder over this basic truth till we are steeped in it. God at his most vitally active and most incarnate is not remote from us, wholly apart from the sphere of the tangible. On the contrary, at every moment he awaits us in the activity, in the work to be done which every moment brings."[57] Total active dedication to God's will in a spirit of loving obedience will presuppose and actually involve a thorough-going asceticism, a self-denial geared to service, and constant mortification.

The fourth and last aspect of a spirituality is finding God in an experiential awareness of the presence of God. This is a sense or perception of God's operative presence in the world or in oneself. It is a gift, a special grace; it is the perfection of faith, and at its highest levels it is mysticism. Pierre Teilhard once wrote, "Lord Jesus, when it was given to me to see where the dazzling trail of particular beauties and partial harmonies was leading, I recognized that it was all coming to a center on a single point, a single person, yourself. Every presence makes me feel that you are near me, every touch is the touch of your hand, every necessity transmits to me a pulsation of your will."[58]

With Teilhard we might pray, "Lord grant that I may see, that I may see you, that I may see and experience you present and animating all things . . . Jesus, help me to perfect the perception and expression of my vision . . . Help me to the right action, the right word, help me to give the example that will reveal you best."[59]

Afterword

SINCE THIS LITTLE BOOK was first published in 1968, several developments in spirituality have occurred to modify and refine its final Teilhardian vision. These developments emphasize an increasingly social perspective rooted in scriptural foundations and aiming at social transformation.

The first development is a renewed interest in the work of the Holy Spirit. At the turn of the twentieth century, Pope Leo XIII prayed the "Come Holy Spirit" for the whole church. At the same time the Rev. Charles Parham and Agnes Ozman prayed for the gift of the Spirit to begin the Holiness Pentecostal Movement. From that beginning the Pentecostal churches grew to become the third largest group of christians after Protestants and Catholics.[60] Around 1957 the Pentecostal movement caught the mainline Protestant churches; and in 1967, shortly after Vatican Council II, it touched a Catholic group at Duquesne University and spread to Notre Dame, Ann Arbor, and then to parish prayer groups all over the United States. Key to its vision is the expectation that God is acting in our day through his Spirit and the charismatic gifts, such as speaking in tongues, prophecy, and healing, just as in the early church. Renewal of the church and the world today depends upon the restoration of the church in God's Holy Spirit through expectant prayer in community. Out of the original prayer groups emerged covenant communities whose full commitment is to spiritual renewal; parish prayer communities also emerged supporting renewal movements in the parishes and in the secular world. The spiritual vision of the Pentecostal movement has also moved from an expansive resurrection spirituality to an increasing focus on the cross and on faithful suffering to bring about the transformation of the world.[61] Where mysticism related individuals to God, charismatic gifts serve whole communities and enable them to stay open to God's direction and empowerment. The charismatic gifts do not imply holiness, any more than ordination or a vocation to marriage or celibacy does, but they lead to holiness if people cooperate with God's grace at work in them.[62]

A second development that has gained momentum in the last fifteen years is liberation theology.[63] Arising in Third World countries plagued by economic injustice and oppression, liberation theology has spread to first world issues of racism, the role of women, and poverty. Again, its focus is on sin and grace in the structures of society, not just on individual morality. It sees Yahweh as a liberating God bringing his enslaved people out of Egypt. It sees Jesus as continuing Yahweh's work by identifying with sinners, the sick, and the outcast, and ultimately facing death with the poor at the hands of the established oppressing powers. From this perspective, work for justice is the main criterion of authentic spirituality; and a person's willingness to suffer for justice reveals God's compassion who in Jesus identifies with the oppressed.[64]

Charismatic spirituality has been accused of neglecting political action for justice, and liberation spirituality has been accused of neglecting prayer. The more recent trend is to unite both prayer and action. Liberation theologians are now advocating a firm grounding in spirituality to support enduring social action against seemingly immovable obstacles.[65] Henri Nouwen has written persuasively of the need first world ministers have of "desert spirituality" if they are not to be coopted into the attitudes of success, popularity, and self-help that pervade our culture.[66]

This need for a spiritual ground in our confusing world is one reason for the popularity of "centering prayer" which christianizes Eastern forms of meditation and retrieves the Orthodox prayer of the heart. By contacting the "still point" within, where one's heart meets God, a person is revivified for liberating work in the world.

Besides these forms of spirituality, two further dimensions now color our understanding of spirituality today: development and healing reconciliation. Traditional spirituality has always implied development: there are the three ways of purgative, illuminative, and unitive prayer that mark progress in the mystical tradition, Teresa of Avila's seven mansions, and Ignatius Loyola's four "weeks" of the Spiritual Exercises. Recent work in developmental psychology and its counterpart in faith development has shown how both social psychology and faith progress from conventional stages, through crises and individual spiritual experiences, to committed creative action.[67] Conventional stages rely on the authority of traditional understandings and traditional role models of spirituality. The individuating stage is based on personal experience and it often evolves into a prophetic challenge to one's tradition, as it did with Jesus. It is this rooting in a personal experience of God that empowers individuals and communities to become committed, creative forces for the transformation of society. It is a vision of God's ongoing creativity that underlies this developmental view of spirituality.

Healing and reconciliation is the second awareness that is becoming clearer in our day.[68] We now see more clearly that it is not just sin that blocks growth in love, but also unconscious wounds received from wounded parents or from personal failures turn us in on ourselves and prevent us from loving. Whereas before we might have considered these wounds a cross we had to live with, experience is now showing that much can be healed. Since God's eternity transcends time, he can touch past wounds of rejection or failure and reveal his loving presence there and draw us into a healing relationship with Jesus and Mary as God's new family. God can also heal divided histories and broken relationships in order to free reconciling love. This healing is precisely why Jesus came in John's view (Jn. 20:21), and this was his commission to his followers; (see also Jn 17:20-21).

Each new dimension of spirituality reveals God in a different light, and every spirituality implies a corresponding view of God. The more developed one is in spirituality, then, the more developed one's view of God will be. Conventional spirituality sees God a rule giver and authority figure. Individuated spirituality begins to see God as inner ground of spiritual growth. And committed self-transcending love sees God as a community of creative self-transcending love. Seen in this light, Jesus' self-surrender on the cross reveals the Father as self-surrendering love, and their joint self-gift releases their Spirit of community-building love in the church.

People in our day can see the need for reconciliation more clearly than ever. We are more aware of the ghosts of fear and hatred that separate nations and threaten nuclear destruction. We are more aware of the divisions that scandalously pervade christianity and those that set clergy against laity, rich against poor, race against race, and women and men against each other. With insight comes a call to heal; and in view of the danger of ultimate destruction, the call to a reconciling spirituality is not merely optional but an absolute necessity for the continued existence of humanity.

As this little book is reissued, a Holy Year of Reconciliation has been proclaimed, and Pope John Paul II has visited several churches to affirm his desire for christian unity despite continuing doctrinal and faith differences. As St. Paul considered himself an ambassador for God who is calling the world to be reconciled to himself (2 Cor. 5:20-21), surely one of the best characteristics of a spirituality for our time is reconciliation, both individual and social.

Robert T. Sears, S.J.
Loyola University of Chicago

Notes

1. Pierre Teilhard de Chardin, S.J., *The Future of Man* (New York: Harper and Row, 1964), p. 12.

2. Quoted in Christopher F. Mooney, S.J., "Ignatian Spirituality and Modern Theology," *Downside Review*, LXXX (1962), 334.

3. Mt. 10:37-38.

4. St. Athanasius, *Life of Anthony*, ch. xiv.

5. Pelagius the Deacon, *Verba Seniorum*, xvii, 5.

6. Hubert Van Zeller, *The Benedictine Ideal* (London: Burns and Oates, 1959), p. 2.

7. On Prayer, #17. Trans. by Elmer O'Brien, *Varieties of Mystic Experience* (New York: Holt, Rinehart and Winston, 1964), p. 61.

8. *Ibid.*, #18. p. 61.

9. *Ibid.*, #61, p. 62.

10. *Ibid.*, #57, p. 62.

11. *Ibid.*, #142. p. 63.

12. Benedictine Monks of St. Meinrad, *The Holy Rule of St. Benedict* (St. Meinrad, Ind.: Grail Press, 1956), p. vii.

13. Hubert Van Zeller, *op. cit.*

14. *The Holy Rule*, p. 85.

15. *Ibid.*, p. 78.

16. Gerard Sitwell, O.S.B., *Spiritual Writers of the Middle Ages* (New York: Hawthorn Books, 1961), p. 21.

17. Ronald Knox, *Enthusiasm* (Oxford: Clarendon Press, 1950), pp. 71-89.

18. Quoted in Josef Pieper, *Guide to Thomas Aquinas* (New York: Pantheon, 1962), p. 23.

19. Quoted in Herbert B. Workman, *The Evolution of the Monastic Ideal* (Boston: Beacon Press, 1962), p. 272.

20. *Little Flowers of St. Francis,* ch. xvi.

21. Thomas a Kempis, *The Imitation of Christ,* I, xix.

22. *Ibid.,* I, x.

23. Thomas Aquinas, *Summa Theologiae,* II-II, q. 188, a. 6.

24. (London: Edward Arnold, 1924), p.1.

25. "Of the most powerful Prayer of all," *The Talks of Instruction.*

26. Quoted by Huizinga, p. 203.

27. *Ibid.*

28. Quoted by O'Brien, p. 151.

29. Huizinga, pp. 136-37.

30. Karl Rahner, S.J., *Visions and Prophesies* (New York: Herder and Herder, 1963), p. 17.

31. *Spiritual Exercises,* #236.

32. Jean Danielou, S.J., "The Ignatian Vision of the Universe and of Man" *Cross Currents,* IV (1954), 364.

33. *Epistola Ignatiana,* VI, 91. Quoted in Giuliani, *Finding God in All Things,* trans. by William J. Young, S.J. (Chicago: Henry Regnery Co., 1958), p. 17.

34. *Ibid.,* p. 11.

35. *Ibid.,* pp. 22-23.

36. *Ibid.,* pp. 8-9.

37. Danielou, *op. cit.*

38. *Ibid.,* p. 366.

39. Hermann Tuchle, "Baroque Christianity: The Root of Triumphalism?" *Historical Problems of Church Renewal,* ed. Roger Aubert (Glen Rock, N.J.: Paulist, 1965), pp. 138-40.

40. *Constitutions,* Pt. VI, ch. iii, 1.

41. *Scripta de S. Ignatio,* I, 515.

42. *Epistolae P. Hieronymi Nadal,* II, 32.

43. Quoted in P. Leturia, S.J. "De oratione matutina in Societate Iesu documenta selecta," *Archivum Historicum S.J.,* III (1934), 102.

44. Heinrich Schlier, *Principalities and Powers in the New Testament* (New York: Herder and Herder, 1961).

45. Translated in *Existentialism from Dostoevsky to Sartre*, ed. Walter Kaufman (New York: Meridian Books, 1963), pp. 287-311.

46. *Spiritual Exercises*, #176.

47. *Ibid.*, #338.

48. *Ibid.*

49. *Letters of St. Ignatius Loyola*, trans. by William J. Young, S.J. (Chicago: Loyola University Press, 1959), p. 22.

50. Bernard Cooke, S.J., Unpublished Proceedings, Santa Clara Conference on Total Jesuit Formation, 1967, III, Pt. 2, p. 162.

51. Teilhard de Chardin, S.J. *The Future of Man*, p. 261.

52. Teilhard de Chardin, S.J. *The Divine Milieu* (New York: Harper and Brothers, 1960), p. 62.

53. Teilhard de Chardin, S.J., *Hymn of the Universe* (New York: Harper and Row, 1965), p. 119.

54. *Ibid.*, p. 149.

55. *Ibid.*, p. 151.

56. *The Divine Milieu*, p. 35.

57. *Hymn of the Universe*, pp. 83-84.

58. *Ibid.*, p. 153.

59. Quoted in Claude Cuenot, *Teilhard de Chardin* (Baltimore: Helicon Press, 1965), p. 374.

60. A recent study from an ecumenical perspective is *The Church is Charismatic*, edited by Arnold Bittlinger (World Council of Churches, 1982). René Laurentin, *Catholic Pentecostalism* (Doubleday, 1977) gives a competent Catholic evaluation.

61. See G. J. Farrell and G. W. Kosicki, *The Spirit and the Bride Say Come* (AMI Press, 1981) pp. 17-20 for the new direction of the movement.

62. A careful theology of the charismatic gifts is by Francis A. Sullivan, *Charism and Charismatic Renewal: A Biblical and Theological Study*, (Servant, 1982).

63. Gustavo Gutierrez, *A Theology of Liberation* (Orbis, 1973) was a path-breaking study for Catholics; and since then many writers like Segundo, Sobrino, Galilea, and Boff have made contributions.

64. Papal Documents have increasingly stressed work for justice as essential to faith. See David Hollenback, *Claims in Conflict*

(Paulist, 1979) for a competent analysis. Several authors have a view of God's suffering as implied in action for justice—Metz, Mühlen, Moltmann, and von Balthasar among others.

65. Gutierrez himself now stresses prayer as essential for work for justice; see his *The Power of the Poor in History*, (Orbis, 1983), pp. 106-7. See also Segundo Galilea, *Following Jesus* (Orbis, 1981) "Following Jesus the Contemplative" p. 45-53.

66. See Henri M. Nouwen, *The Way of the Heart: Desert Spirituality and Contemporary Ministry* (Seabury, 1981).

67. John H. Westerhoff, *Will Our Children Have Faith?* (Seabury, 1976) and James W. Fowler, *Stages of Faith* (Harper and Row, 1981) have both written on faith development. I have developed a communal view of spiritual growth in light of the Trinity in "Trinitarian Love as Ground of the Church," *Theological Studies*, Dec. 1976, pp. 652-679.

68. Matthew and Dennis Linn and Sheila Fabricant, *Prayer Course for Healing Life's Hurts*, (Paulist, 1983) have made available practical steps for healing including healing for social action. They give relevant further bibliography for additional study.

CHRISTIAN SPIRITUALITY:
A Schematic Chronology

A.D.
4

Birth of Jesus Christ

Pauline writings
Synoptic narratives

100 ——————————————————————————————————————

Johannine writings

Tertullian

200 ——————————————————————————————————————

Origen ◄——————— Plotinus

300 ——————————————————————————————————————

Anthony, Pachomius (Coptic line)
Athanasius

BASIL
Origenism: Evagrius
(Alexandrian line)
Augustine   Cassian ◄——— Cassian

400 ——————————————————————————————————————

500 ——————————————————————————————————————

BENEDICT   Pseudo-Dionysius

600 ——————————————————————————————————————

Benedictine
Missionary movement

700 ——————————————————————————————————————

Benedictine
Governmental reforms
(Benedict of Aniane)

800 ———————————————————————————————————

900 ———————————————————————————————————

Cluniac Reform

1000 ——————————————————————————————————

Camaldolese (Eremitic movement)
Vallombrosians (Cenobitic movement)
Carthusians (Bruno)
Cistertians (Robert, Stephen Harding)

1100 ——————————————————————————————————

Canons of AUGUSTINE   Bernard (Clairvaux)
(Branches: Canons of St.
Victor, Premonstr., etc.)
    —Military Orders

                    Benedictine   Hildegard, Mechtilde,
                    Visionaries: Gertrude

1200 ——————————————————————————————————

        Mendicants:

Dominic   Francis   [Carmelites]
Thomas Aquinas   Spirituals vs. Observants
                        Bonaventure

1300 ——————————————————————————————————

Rhineland mystics: *English mystics:*

    Eckhart   Rolle, Hilton
    Tauler, Suso   "Cloud of Unknowing"
    Ruysbroeck   Julian of Norwich
        Groote

1400 ——————————————————————————————————

            Thomas a Kempis

        Garcia de Cisneros

1500 ——————————————————————————————————

IGNATIUS   Other *Spanish mystics:*
                        Teresa of Avila
        Borgia   John of the Cross

                            Vincent de Paul
                            Francis de Sales

```
1600 ─────────────────────────────────────────────

        Aquaviva
          Lallement
                          Quietism (Fénélon vs. Bossuet)
                          Jansenism—Margaret Mary
                                      Colombière—Croiset
                                      Other Jesuit writers
1700 ─────────────────────────────────────────────

        DeCaussade           Alphonsus Liguori (Redemptorists)
                             Paul of the Cross (Passionists)

        Supression of Society of Jesus

1800 ─────────────────────────────────────────────

        Restoration of S.J.: Roothaan

                    Oxford movement: Newman
                    Victorian piety: Faber
                    French spirituality: Lacordaire, Vianney
                                    Ozanam (rise of the layman)
                    Revival of theology in Germany (Scheeben)

1900 ─────────────────────────────────────────────

        M. -J. Lagrange          Marmion          Mercier
        Blondel, Teilhard de Chardin               Maréchal
        DeLubac, Daniélou                          Guardini
                                                   Rahner
```